D0952585

The
Heart
Aroused

CURRENCY

DOUBLEDAY

New York London Toronto
Sydney Auckland

The Heart Aroused

▼

*Poetry and the
Preservation of the Soul
in Corporate America*

DAVID WHYTE

A CURRENCY BOOK
PUBLISHED BY DOUBLEDAY

a division of Bantam Doubleday Dell Publishing Group, Inc.
1540 Broadway, New York, New York 10036

CURRENCY and DOUBLEDAY are trademarks of Doubleday, a division of
Bantam Doubleday Dell Publishing Group, Inc.

Permissions to reprint previously published material can be found on
pages 305–7.

Book design by Chris Welch

Library of Congress Cataloging-in-Publication Data
Whyte, David.
The heart aroused : poetry and the preservation of the soul
in corporate America / David Whyte. — 1st ed.
p.   cm.
1. Success.   2. Self-actualization (Psychology)
3. Conduct of life.   4. Quality of work life.
I. Title.
BF637.S8W46   1994
158'.1—dc20
93-50562
CIP
ISBN 0-385-42350-0

Only a few achieve the colossal task of holding together, without being split asunder, the clarity of their vision alongside an ability to take their place in a materialistic world. They are the modern heroes. . . . Artists at least have a form within which they can hold their own conflicting opposites together. But there are some who have no recognized artistic form to serve this purpose, they are artists of the living. To my mind these last are the supreme heroes in our soulless society.

—IRENE CLAREMONT DE CASTILLEJO

For Peter and Joel,
friends, teachers, colleagues, and fellow travelers

Acknowledgments

To Autumn, who is, among her many talents, a sure and instinctive editorial consultant, and who with my son Brendan provided understanding, endless cups of tea, and a patience I do not deserve. To Peter Block for his sudden, surprising, and imaginative invitation to work in corporate America, to Joel Henning for his stories and his passion, to them both for marvelous inspiration and good company at the dinner table. To all my fine friends and colleagues at Designed Learning, to Bennett White for his sure friendship and listening ear, to Edward Wates and Will Prestwood for companionship on the Cumbrian hills, single malt in the farmhouse at Roger Ground, and their close reading and comments. To Dana Gioia for his fine and provocative essay, to my assistant, Julie Quiring, whose efficiency is matched only by her patience and who endured constant status reports whether she wished for them or not, to Priya for her resourceful help with permissions, to my agent Ned Leavitt, who has a wisdom and humanity even greater than his talents as a literary agent, and lastly to my two editors at Doubleday, Harriet Rubin, who played Fury to my Muse and made the book far better than anything I could have achieved alone, and Janet Coleman, who displayed a sure touch in the closing stages. All the above have contributed to whatever qualities the book may have; its many flaws and omissions are entirely my own.

Contents

The Path Begins

Inviting the Soul to Work

In the middle of the road of my life I awoke

in a dark wood where the true way was

wholly lost —DANTE, COMMEDIA

T *he Heart Aroused* attempts to keep what is tried and true, good and efficient, at the center of our present work life, while opening ourselves to a mature appreciation of the hidden and often dangerous inner seas where our passions and our creativity lie waiting.

Much of this book deals with the hidden and neglected side of corporate life, where a woman's or a man's soul has been forced to reside, like Tolkien's character Gollum, in dark and subterranean caves. Modern business life arises from a love of the upper world, of material products, of order and organization; it celebrates the material, light-filled portion of existence. It is the world as we see it (or as we would like to see it) and as it most makes sense to us. It has been the basis of our Western affluence, and by the life it has provided many of us in the West, it has much to recommend it. But as many of us suspect, sensing the shock waves now traveling through our corporations and institutions, it is only half the story.

If this book has a tremorlike quality, it may stem from its geological investigation of the shifting ground upon which we now stand every day at work.

The Heart Aroused is written for those who have chosen to live out their lives as managers and employees
of a postmodern Corporate America, and who struggle to keep their humanity in the process. The book
stands or fails upon its ability to work with what
Wordsworth called

> *. . . a dark invisible workmanship*
> *that reconciles discordant elements*
> *and makes them move in one society*

Not because what is dark and invisible is necessarily
better, but because it is not now *joined* to what is light
and visible to us every day in the corporate world. It
has been pushed away and ignored. This split between our work life and that part of our soul life
forced underground seems to be at the root of much
of our current unhappiness. This book attempts to
look at the stress this split causes in the human psyche
and the way the soul attempts to heal and preserve its
life amid the pressures of schedule and ambition.

But this healing is not a simple recipe for a happy
work life. There are energies and powers in the world
that are greater than any human endeavor, even the
mighty corporate world that we hold in so much es-
teem. Despite everything our inheritance may tell us,
work is not and never has been the very center of the
human universe; and the universe, with marvelous
compassion, seems willing to take endless pains to
remind us of that fact. Once basic necessities are

taken care of, there are other more immediate urgencies central to human experience, and it is these urgencies that are continually breaking through our fondest hopes for an ordered work life. The split between what is nourishing at work and what is agonizing is the very chasm from which our personal destiny emerges. Accepting the presence of this chasm we can begin to deal, one step at a time, with the continually hidden, underground forces that shape our lives, often against our will.

The field of human creativity has long been a constant battleground between the upper world we inhabit every day and the deeper untrammeled energies alive in every element of life. Camille Paglia has written brilliantly on this tumultuous relationship between the two worlds, one seen everyday, the other half-hidden, in her recent book *Sexual Personae*. Tracing a line from ancient Egypt to contemporary popular society, she investigates the way artists and poets have long seen the deeper uncharted territory in the human psyche as a subterranean landscape they wish to describe, map, and bring to light. The world of commerce has, until now, run a mile from this hidden world; organizations have more often seen these underground and seemingly eccentric desires as a source of continual interruption into their production and purpose. This is now changing. Continually calling on its managers and line workers for more creativity, dedication, and adaptability, the American corporate world is tiptoeing for the first time in its very short history into the very place from whence that dedication, creativity, and adaptability must come: the turbulent place where the soul of an individual is formed and finds expression.

These first tentative corporate steps toward understanding personal artistry and individual creativity are bringing to life a swirling natural boundary where human beings have always lived uneasily; one foot planted solidly in the light-filled world, the other desperately looking for purchase in the dark unknown. Whether we spend our days as an artist painting in a studio-garret in Greenwich Village or as a manager in the streamlined lineaments of the modern office, we are subject to the roiling interplay between these worlds. Despite our best hopes for ourselves and for humanity, this other, hidden energy is constantly welling up from the very ground of existence. The ancient Aegean civilizations called this hidden, ever-present dynamic the Dionysian.

In preclassical Greek thought, the light-filled part of existence was represented by Apollo. If we want to imagine the Apollonic in our lives it might be to think of ourselves, one August day, whistling happily as we work, painting a white picket fence in Dade County, Florida, proud of our home and our plans and happy that God is in his heaven. The Dionysian is Hurricane Andrew the very next day, blowing your fence, your house, and your kids' future, without qualm or conscience, off God's green earth.

It is the part of life that carries passion, sound, and

fury, or frightening emptiness, and often no immediate meaning outside of the cruel. It is the part of life
at which we might gladly shake our fist. It is Job la-
menting at the perfidy of God's justice. It is everything we were afraid could be true about existence,
and astonishingly, and despite everything we would
wish to the contrary, it seems to be an energy without
which we cannot appreciate the gift of the light-filled,
ordered world; remove it, and our soul life becomes
puzzlingly empty and impoverished.

Yet the sound and the fury of an individual's creative life are the elemental waters missing from the
dehydrated workday. The frightening emptiness of
existence also contains a place of nourishment and
repose, a blessed opportunity for calm at the center
of the corporate whirlwind. From the organizational
side, if the corporations ignore the darker underbelly
of their employees' lives for a well-meaning approach, emphasizing only the positive, they will be
forced to rely on expensive management pyramids to
manipulate their workers at the price of commitment. Adaptability and native creativity on the part
of the workforce come through the door only with
their passions. Their passions come only with their
souls. Their souls love the hidden springs boiling and
welling at the center of existence more than they love
the company.

Taking a step toward soul life during the full light
of the workday, we begin a journey toward a subterranean world that until now we have only explored

after-hours, during the drive home, or in the silence of the small hours. Like any journey into neglected places, this journey has a natural drama to it. The cost of failure, as I point out in the stories and poetry that follow, is very high, but the prize is an experience of work that can benefit the spirit as much as the pocket, a nourishing approach to work that may make the moment equally as fulfilling as the years of patient sacrifice.

THE POET AND THE CORPORATION

As a poet, I did not foresee myself working in corporate America, a world I was taught to view with suspicion by a solid, almost nineteenth-century upbringing in the north of England. Still, when asked, I could not resist the first invitation to bring poetry to bear on certain aspects of change and creativity now being confronted in the workplace. I expected to be at least a little corrupted by my immersion, but in the process discovered as much about my own arrogance as that of the American corporation. Over the last years of working with companies of all sizes and descriptions, I have tried to illuminate specific steps along the path of change, and the forces that work for and against an individual who asks for more commitment and passion in his work. Rather than talking *about* change, I use hundreds of memorized poems to try to bring to life the *experience* of change itself. Doing this, I have had seven humbling years in which I have been forced to drop, one by one, many of the prejudices against the corporate world my personal history had generously provided me. I found my image of contemporary business as outdated and clichéd as the business world's image of my own world of poetry and poets.

The poet was led to believe that *they*, the business people, were a faceless conformist hierarchy busily destroying the world while doomed to a life of ineffable blandness. *We* poets, so business people told themselves, were all either starving in garrets or living comfortably in academic ivory towers, dreaming away our lives, contributing nothing to the practical matters of the world.

There *are* bland, faceless, and exploitative corporations, and there *are* starving, curmudgeonly, or academic poets unwilling to come to terms with the greater realities of existence, but both are the vestigial remains of a world that I for one would be glad to see disappear. The poet needs the practicalities of making a living to test and temper the lyricism of insight and observation. The corporation needs the poet's insight and powers of attention in order to weave the inner world of soul and creativity with the outer world of form and matter. The meeting of those two worlds forms the very heart of this book.

The poet has always suspected that we live in an unfathomable, shape-shifting world that must be lived and experienced rather than controlled or solved, but the poet has often relinquished personal power because of deep worries about the misuses of patriarchal power. Poets have often chosen the seemingly safer path of refusing to act at all and in the very process disenfranchised themselves from a messy world which, unfairly, still calls for clear-cut decisions.

The corporations, for their part, have been engaged in a willful battle against the very grain of existence. Like the good Dutch boy with his finger in the dike, they have spent enormous amounts of energy putting in place systems that attempt to hold back the shifting oceanic qualities of existence. The complexity of the world could be accounted for, they fervently hoped, by a simple increase in the thickness of the company manual.

The Heart Aroused is written to bring the insights of the poetic imagination out of the garret and into the boardrooms and factory floors of America. Corporate America desperately needs the powers historically associated with the poetic imagination not only to see their way through the present whirligig of change, but also, because poetry asks for accountability to a human community, for rootedness and responsibility even as it changes.

The twenty-first century will be anything but *business as usual*. Institutions must now balance the need to make a living with a natural ability to change. They must also honor the souls of the individuals who work for them and the great soul of the natural world from which they take their resources.

But finding the soul in American corporate life is blessedly fraught with difficulties. The seething, snapping, boisterously self-referential American way of business is like American life itself, at once a gift and a tempting poison. Facing the invitation to write this book, I grew fainthearted at the prospect of melding the fluid language of the soul with the dehydrated jargon of the modern workplace. A large part of me simply wanted to wave the challenge good-bye and do what I do best—stay in my own world, writing and performing poetry. Yet as one of few contemporary poets working in the corporate world, I felt a responsibility to at least attempt it. Two events finally convinced me to take it on.

First came a beautifully written, front-page article in the *Atlantic Monthly* by the poet Dana Gioia, calling on contemporary poets to rise out of their self-referential world and bring their talents back into the mainstream of American society. Gioia's essay had a profound impact on many poets; it forced them to see themselves in a far wider context, a context that asked for more participation than the poet's tradition as outsider usually allowed.

But the more telling moment of decision came on a visit to my local bank to get a construction loan for, of all things, a new writing studio. I knew the manager well from previous business, and he knew something of my work. He had always struck me as a cheerful and very vital man, but that morning he looked exhausted. His desk was filled from one corner to another with memos, notes, blinking telephones, and piles of forms and loan applications. Greeting me, he looked as if he carried the weight of the world on his shoulders.

Seemingly tired of this existence he waved his arm vaguely over the array of pressing details and began to ask me questions about my work as a poet. After a brief tour of my travels, he asked me if I was presently working on a book. "Well," I said, "I haven't written a word, but someone, for heaven's sake, wants me to write about the *life of the soul* in corporate America." There was a moment's pause, then he leaned across the desk, placed his hand on mine for the briefest of instants, and with the weariest and most soulful look I could imagine said, *"Tell me about it."* I looked at him, nodded back wearily and said nothing. Inside I felt something rise up; almost against my will, I heard myself saying, *"Ask me like that,* and I *will* tell you about it."

The Heart Aroused is dedicated to that weary questioner and all others like him, myself included, struggling with the increasing complexity of the modern workplace. Work is struggle. It mostly *has* been struggle, it mostly *will* be struggle. If we are to talk about soul life and work life, we are not speaking of some Elysian field where we can lie down and rest. There *is* in work, in the ancient sense, a dustless place, a place to find rest and repose, but the soul's attempts to find home and rest in work can be done only by accounting for and living through the chaotic battle-ground of everyday existence. As Wallace Stevens said in his "Reply to Papini":

> *The way through the world*
> *Is more difficult to find than the way beyond it.*

Any man or woman working in the pressure of a modern corporation is making their way *through* the world, but it may be a world that seems, as the years roll by, to have less and less room for soul.

SOUL

But what is soul, and what is meant by the preservation of the soul? By definition, soul evades the cage of definition. It is the *indefinable* essence of a person's spirit and being. It can never be touched and yet the merest hint of its absence causes immediate distress. In a work situation, its lack can be sensed intuitively, though a person may, at the same moment, be power-less to know what has caused the loss. It may be the transfer of a well-loved colleague to another depart-ment, a change of rooms to a less appealing office, or, more seriously, the inner intuitions of a path not taken. Though the *Oxford English Dictionary*'s lofty attempt at soul is *the principle of life in man or ani-*

mals, depth-psychologist James Hillman describes it in far more eloquent terms in his provocative book of selected writings, A *Blue Fire:*

To understand *soul* we cannot turn to science for a description. Its meaning is best given by its context . . . words long associated with the soul amplify it further: mind, spirit, heart, life, warmth, humanness, personality, individuality, intentionality, essence, innermost purpose, emotion, quality, virtue, morality, sin, wisdom, death, God. A soul is said to be "troubled," "old," "disembodied," "immortal," "lost," "innocent," "inspired." Eyes are said to be "soulless" by showing no mercy. The soul has been imaged as . . . given by God and thus divine, as conscience, as a multiplicity and as a unity in diversity, as a harmony, as a fluid, as fire, as dynamic energy, and so on . . . the search for the soul leads always into the "depths."

Entering the "depths" and entering a corporate workplace are rarely seen in the same light. Looking over the vast amount of management literature, very few authors are willing to take the soul seriously in the workplace. The soul's needs in the workplace have long been ignored, partly because the path the soul takes to fulfill its destiny seems troublesomely unique to each person and refuses to be quantified in a way that satisfies our need to plan everything in advance.

The Heart Aroused will look at the link between soul and creativity, success and failure, efficiency and malaise at work, but it sets as its benchmark not the fiscal success of the work or the corporation (though this certainly can be good for the soul), but the journey and experience of the human spirit and its repressed but unflagging desire to find a home in the world. It is written not only to meet the ancient human longing for meaning in work, but also in celebration of the natural human irreverence for work's authoritarian, all-encompassing dominance of our present existence.

Preservation of the soul means the preservation at work of humanity and sanity (with all the well-loved insanities that human sanity requires). Preservation of the soul means the palpable presence of some sacred otherness in our labors, whatever language we may use for that otherness: God, the universe, destiny, life, or love. Preservation of the soul means allowing for fiery initiations that our surface personalities, calculating for a brilliant career, would rather do without.

Yevgeny Yevtushenko says:

> *Sorrow happens, hardship happens,*
> *the hell with it, who never knew*
> *the price of happiness, will not be happy*

> Trans. Peter Levi

Preservation of the soul means giving up our wish, in the scheduled workplace, for immunity from the unscheduled meeting with sorrow and hardship. It means learning the price of happiness. Preservation of the soul means refusing to relinquish the body and its sensual appreciation of texture, color, multiplicity, pain, and joy. Above all, preserving the soul means preserving a desire to live a life a man or woman can truly call their own.

For consultants and management gurus, the soul is a slippery customer. On the one hand it may be dismissed completely. Many trainers and consultants maintain that the soul belongs at home or in church. But with little understanding of the essential link between the soul life and the creative gifts of their employees, hardheaded businesses listening so carefully to their hardheaded consultants may go the way of the incredibly hardheaded dinosaurs. For all their emphasis on the bottom line, they are adrift from the very engine at the center of a person's creative application to work, they cultivate a workforce unable to respond with personal artistry to the confusion of global market change.

On the other hand, many progressive management gurus ask that the person's soul life be included fully in their work but imagine that the vast, hidden Dionysian underworld of the soul erupting into everyday work life can only be positive. The darker side of human energy is very often sanitized and explained away as the product of bad work environments. Change the environment, they say, and all good things will fall into place, but this displays an untested middle class faith in the innate goodness of humanity that is only partially true, one doomed to fail when faced with the terrifying necessity of the soul to break, if necessary, every taboo, and wend its vital way onward, irrespective of family, corporation, deadline, or career.

This book does not offer easy answers as to the way that home life and work life, career and creativity, soul life and seniority, can be brought together. What it does do is chart a veritable San Andreas Fault in the modern American psyche: the personality's wish to have power *over* experience, to control all events and consequences, and the soul's wish to have power *through* experience, *no matter what that may be*. It offers the poet's perspective on the way men and women throughout history have lived triumphantly or tragically through both their daily work and their life's work. For the personality, bankruptcy or failure may be a disaster, for the soul it may be grist for its strangely joyful mill and a condition it has been secretly engineering for years.

I use poetry to chart this difficult fault line in the human psyche not because the fault line is vague and woolly, but because, like human nature, it is dramatic and multidimensional, yet strangely precise. No language matches good poetry in its precision about the human drama. "My heart rouses," says William Carlos Williams (generously giving me, by way of Dana Gioia's article, the title of this book) "thinking to bring you news of something that concerns you and concerns many men."

My heart rouses
          thinking to bring you news
               of something
that concerns you
          and concerns many men. Look at
               what passes for the new.
You will not find it there but in
          despised poems.
               It is difficult
to get the news from poems
          yet men die miserably every day
               for lack
of what is found there.

"Look at what passes for the new. You will not find it there . . ." None of the thought processes that have been brought to bear on the individual working in a modern organization have the rigor of poetry in dealing with the cussed, not-to-be-believed, patterned chaos of the human soul going through the average workday or a life's career. "Yet men die miserably every day for lack of what is found there."

THE DIFFICULTY AND DRAMA
OF WORK

Work is drama, and our inability to live vitally upon its stage has as much to do with the modern loss of dramatic sensibility, the lost sense that we play out our lives as part of a greater story, as it does with the acknowledged alienation of the twentieth-century work environment. To quote a Shakespearean cliché, repeated to death because it is so stubbornly true: *All the world's a stage.* Work is theater, the place where life unfolds to our tragic or comic satisfaction.

Through drama we find that poetry and myth, the operative tools of this book, grant meaning even to failure. Drama is vital, quirky, humorous, tragic, and by its playing out of the stuff of life, lends magnificence to the commonplace. Myth is the greater story of which we are a part, without which the commonplace becomes a burden.

Work *is* the commonplace and feeds the enormous need in humans for getting things done; but also for money, respect, community, conflict, meaning, and spectacle. Spectacle? Witness Oliver Stone's loving camera panning the frenzied brokers and their vital, exhausting work environments in *Wall Street*; or recall *It's a Wonderful Life*, the old forties movie, with James Stewart picturesquely jammed into a small-town office. Look up, next time you are downtown, at the highest floors and see the towering, cinematically splendid, almost Egyptian seclusion of upper corporate officers. Across the Atlantic, I vividly remember an astonishing wall of London commuters, recently released from a jammed train, advancing across Tower Bridge like an angry tsunami.

In drama, as at work, the stakes are always high. We take a chance every day, whether it be the intense and elaborate engineering of a collective laugh, or the gut-wrenching presentation of financial loss. Our nervous laughter at the prospect of being fired encompasses both. Our mouth turns dry at the very thought.

In work, the stakes are *dramatically* high. You *can* be fired today, this very moment. Your company *can* go under. Even if it seems as invulnerable as the *Titanic*, *you* may be busily and efficiently rearranging the deck chairs even as it disappears beneath the waves. Loutish and brutal takeover specialists may break in through the back door, take over the company, break it up, and sell it off for breathtaking personal gain. Your husband may hate your job and ask you to give it up, your wife may leave you because of your unstoppable, Faustian worship of career. Like drama, everything is at stake and everything can happen, and real human souls are living at the center of it all.

If work is all about *doing*, then the soul is all about *being*: the indiscriminate enjoyer of everything that comes our way. If work is the world, then the soul is our home. This book explores the possibility of being at home in the world, melding soul life with work life, the inner ocean of longing and belonging with the outer ground of strategy and organizational control. Its aim is to reconcile the left-hand ledger sheet of the soul with the right-hand ledger sheet of the corporate world, a kind of double-entry bookkeeping that can bring together two opposing sides of ourselves normally split by the pressures of work.

The time seems right for this cross-fertilization. It seems that all the overripe hierarchies of the world, from corporations to nation states, are in trouble and are calling, however reluctantly, on their people for more creativity, commitment, and innovation. If these corporate bodies can demand those creative qualities which by long tradition belong so directly to our being, to our soul, they must naturally make room for their disturbing presence within their buildings and their borders. But the human ability to innovate and follow an individual vision depends also on a sure foundation of continuity and community. The corporation must make room for an equally strong need for stability and tradition, reverence and respect, continuity and contemplation. Above all, the corporation demanding creativity from its own employees has as much changing to do as their workforce. Like water flowing from an underground spring, human creativity is the wellspring greening the desert of toil and effort, and much of what stifles us in the workplace is the immense unconscious effort on the part of individuals and organizations alike to dam its flow.

WORK AND THE SOUL

Work has to do with cornering and controlling conscious life. It attempts concrete goals. It loves the linear and the defined. But the soul finds its existence through a loss of control to those powers greater than human experience.

Work helps us to feel safe. The soul *is* safe already. Safe in its own experience of the world. Work is bounded by time. The soul of a person lies outside of time and belongs to the unknown, it is the sacred *otherness* of existence. Work belongs to the personality, but the soul is owned by no one, not even by the personality formed around it. The personality will, we are continually amazed, kiss any required part of the anatomy to rise in the world; the soul refuses to kiss anything but life itself, and then, as Blake says, only *as it flies*.

Work is slowly mastered. The soul life of a person is always larger and greater the more we come to know it. We *go* to work. But it is our *soul* we put into it. Work is a series of events. The soul, as James Hillman says, turns those workaday events into *experience*.

Our lack of soul is our refusal to open to a full experience of the world. Work, paradoxically, does not ask enough of us, yet exhausts the narrow parts of us we do bring to its door. Old notions of the virtue of work for its own sake are coming into question; in some ways the world is dying from our willingness to work at all and at any cost. Presented every day with the degradation of earth, sea and atmosphere through our virtuous effort, we have enough evidence to suppose now that work itself may mean a further tearing at the fabric of life. The soul must often live and work in places we have made more and more inimical to its desires.

The core of difficulty at the heart of modern work life is its abstraction from many of the ancient cycles of life that allow the silence and time in which true appreciation and experience can take place. The hurried child becomes the pressured student, and finally the harassed manager. The process is begun very young, and can be so in our bones, depending on the pressure of our upbringing, that the inability to pay real attention to our world may be difficult to recognize.

TURNING OFF THE PATH

For many of us, it is hard to begin the soul's journey because the journey begins in a place in which we have been taught to have very little faith—the black, contemplative splendors of self-doubt, something else they don't teach at Harvard Business School and something we would rather do without. But wanting soul life without the dark, warming intelligence of personal doubt is like expecting an egg without the brooding heat of the mother hen.

Self-doubt is that part of the soul that is able to taste the bitter in life as well as the sweet. It is open to a side of life that a sunny disposition must ignore in order to carry on smiling. It is less interested in pretence and more aware of the suffering entailed in daily living. It is realistic about the balance of suffering and happiness, but because of this realism is willing to be thankful for whatever genuine happiness is possible. It celebrates the melancholy nature of aloneness, but because of its refusal to shirk aloneness knows the worth of a real relationship.

The whole of western cultural tradition is based on a primary interior struggle: the essential aloneness of the individual, coupled with a wish to be part of some larger corporate body—literally a *corpus*, a *corporation*—to achieve things that would be impossible alone. Bridging two impossible worlds, personal destiny and impersonal organization, we find ourselves standing in a half-dark, twilight land between them both.

As we begin to think about our aloneness, where we fit in the world, why we are working where we are, the state of our soul and the direction we are headed, we join a long lineage of men and women who gave themselves over to the imagery of the poetic imagination to find out the selfsame thing. We begin to give those images life by speaking them aloud, however hesitantly. Questioning in a real way, we start, by all the lights of the poetic tradition, *to awaken*. We are come to consciousness, albeit in a dark wood. But as we awaken, we take the first steps into the hall of grief and loss. Looking over the centuries of human struggle commemorated in poetry, a man or woman often seems to begin the journey to soul recovery in this very lonely place of self-assessment. The uninitiated might call it depression.

When all the things we want *beyond* our reach move slowly *within* our reach, it is easy to feel good about life. But if our sense of well-being becomes dependent on the constant delivery of goods to our door, we experience a sense of loss when the supply suddenly dries up, or we no longer perceive it has the same value. At this point we are thrown back on ourselves and must live on what we find there. In a way we are finally forced to rely on the one thing already within the compass of our grasp—our soul's natural entanglement in the world. This entanglement is often perceived for the first time through a sense of loss. It is as if we first stumble into our belonging by realizing how desperately out of place we feel. This sense of loss has a natural way of drawing us inside ourself. We might at first label the body's simple need to focus inward depression. But as we practice going inward, we come to realize that much of it is not depression in the least; it is a cry for something else, often the physical body's simple need for rest, for contemplation, and for a kind of forgotten courage, one difficult to hear, demanding not a raise, but another life.

It seems that to find the real path we have to go *off* the path we are on now, even for an instant, and earn the privilege of losing our way. As the path fades, we are forced to take a good look at the life in which we actually find ourselves. For many professionals in the corporate world, going off the path may simply mean approaching work in a more contemplative way, that is, to meditate on work's problems as much with the heart as with the mind. This is not to give up our responsibilities and the need to get a job done on time, but to see things from a radical perspective. Imaginative decision-making means being able to step out of the process at hand and see it with fresh, leisurely eyes. Equally so for the *life* of the imagination.

All goals, mission statements, positive thinking, bonus mileage plans, and future career moves safely to the rear, we can look around and find ourselves, slightly chilled, in a small, unfamiliar clearing in a dark wood, facing that stubborn, unremitting, not-to-be-accepted *life* we have made and must call our own. One day, *Nel mezzo*, in the middle of everything, we awake and see our life as we have made it.

Seven centuries ago, Dante Alighieri began his magisterial epic on existence, the *Commedia*, with these words.

> *In the middle of the road of my life*
> *I awoke in a dark wood*
> *where the true way was wholly lost.*

In the wild and emphatic vowel sounds of medieval Italian, Dante's first line carries the impact of a speeding jetliner, after long flight, jolting to earth on a foreign runway. *Nel mezzo . . . del cammin . . . de*

nostra vita . . . mi retrovai . . . per un oscure selva.
"In the middle . . . of the road . . . of my life . . . I
awoke . . . in a dark wood."

Once landed and down the jetway, we find the ter-
minal strangely empty and in complete darkness. Not
only that, but as in a dream we realize that we were
the sole passenger on the plane. For Dante it was the
midpoint of his life, around thirty-five. For many of
us it can be a particular year or a particular moment.
The twentieth-century manager suddenly looks up
through her Manhattan window and watches the can-
yons of vertical concrete through long forgotten eyes,
seeing suddenly, as Dante saw, the dark trunks of an
unknown forest.

In three brief lines Dante says that the journey
begins right here. In the middle of the road. Right
beneath your feet. This is the place. There is no
other place and no other time. Even if you are
successful and follow the road you have set yourself, you can never leave *here*. Despite everything
you have achieved, life refuses to grant you, and
always will refuse to grant you, immunity from
its difficulties.

Becoming aware of this after a lifetime of accepting success as the ultimate healing balm, as
something that will give you protection, is, declares
Dante, like waking in a dark wood. He begins by admitting that the human mind never sees success as
"here," but always ahead, down the road. He says that
the day when you have your desk finally cleared will

not arrive. That the level of safety you are aiming for on the corporate ladder is an illusion. He says the child you have at home, for whom you are making many sacrifices, will be grown and gone by the time you struggle back through the traffic. He says you must look hard at the road you are taking now as much as the hoped-for destination. You must admit what you see on that road and grieve long for what you do not. Then you have a possibility of waking.

When you do wake, you are rousing a different part of you, a barely experienced life that lies at your core. Having forgotten this central soul experience, you do not recognize where you are. To the part of you that loved your sleep, it feels as if it is waking in the dark. It appears to be lost.

> I awoke in a dark wood
> where the true way was wholly lost.

Little wonder that invoking the soul at work may lead us to feel we are inviting in a dark interior energy over which we have little control. The image may be of a shadowy wood, it may equally feel like a return to the waters of the womb. We feel a panicky sense of being smothered by the mothering energy of the world, as if we might drown if we attempted to enter.

The mythopoetic tradition, the tradition of story and myth telling through poetry, has always said *yes*, this *is* a frightening interior energy that has far fewer boundaries than we are used to, but you must nevertheless enter the waters and be reborn, or die of paralysis on the banks of the pool. William Blake always maintained that the true man was the twice-born man. That is, the mature person was one who had entered the oceanic qualities of the soul and survived that baptism without regressing to a spontaneous but fearful second childhood.

We are all aware how work both emboldens us and strangles our soul life in the very same instant. It reveals how much we can do as part of a larger body, literally a corpus, a *corporation*, and how much the wellsprings of our creativity are stopped at the source by the pressures of that same smothering organization.

These inner wellsprings form deep pools of soul energy within us. For many of us, it has been difficult to allow ourselves to drink from them. We know intuitively that the first sip of intoxicating revelation is bought at very great cost. As if in preparation, the strategic part of our mind has already done a thorough cost-benefit analysis and is advising us not to go through with the bargain.

We experience a form of internal sticker-shock, that the price of our vitality is the sum of all our fears, that the price of our passion and commitment involves the shattering of deep personal illusions of immunity and safety. We stand to gain a marvelous involvement in our labors, but must relinquish a belief that the world owes us a place on a divinely ordained career ladder. We learn that we do have a place in the world, but that it is constantly shape-shifting, like the weather and the seasons, into something at once new and beautiful, tantalizing and terrible.

Confronted with the difficulty and drama of work, we look into our lives as we look into deep water. We kneel, as if by the side of a pool, seeing in one moment not only the fleeting and gossamer reflection of our own face, clouded and disturbed by every passing breath and the lives of all the innumerable creatures that live in its waters, but the hidden depths below, beyond our sight, sustaining and holding everything we comprehend.

Beowulf

Power and Vulnerability in the Workplace

No man or woman, standing at the edge of their own inner pool of darkness, is exempt from the wish to pass by this stage, to find a safe, dry land bridge and walk across. We intuit in those waters the potentialities and dreams of a lifetime, but, finding them hidden by the strangely irrational depth of our fear, we are not sure they are worth the grief.

Besides, our fine professional clothes were not designed for entering uncharted and muddy depths. In the business world there are anxieties enough without adding to them. Appearances are paramount, there is very little tolerance for downtime. The Koreans and the Japanese are not great readers of Jungian psychology and will have another product on the shelves before we have surfaced for air. There are things we also feel good about—the relief from other people's emotional burdens in a professional environment can be refreshing. We feel reluctant to let our own unresolved problems continually wash over our colleagues.

But human existence is half light and half dark, and our creative possibilities seem strangely linked to that part of us we keep in the dark. Trying to bring out our creativity in the workplace, we suddenly realize how unwelcoming a professional corporate setting can be to the darker soul struggles of human existence. But simply turning away from these shadows, no matter how professional our environment, does not mean that they cease to exist. Many organizationally impressive regimes, such as the nuclear power industry, have attempted to be impeccably professional and well run on the surface, but, hobbled by an untrammeled belief in their technology, they are more often rabidly superstitious and on the high road to disaster at the core. For example, we know of no civilization that has lasted longer than a *few* thousand years. Yet we propose to bury radioactive waste that will still be dangerous over *one hundred thousand years* from now. This can only be a product of what psychologists call Magical Thinking, the belief that somehow we will be exempted from the griefs and losses that have afflicted others and that somehow, because of our special knowledge, we will be protected.

Refusing to admit the more elemental energies of the human psyche because of narrow interpretations of what is professional, we construct, in effect, a kind of internal pressurized reactor, where poisonous leakage is simply a matter of time and human error. Sooner or later the trapped energies will emerge and run our lives in unconscious ways. But we live in a forlorn hope that we can keep it all trapped and contained forever.

The spectrum of human response to this containment is very wide. We may, like the Hanford Reservation in Washington State, emit invisible, poisonous leaks over many years, poisoning the local population, only admitting much later, or perhaps never admitting, the full measure of damage. Or more seriously, if the individual is unstable, we might experience a catastrophic meltdown of the system, a Chernobyl of the inner psyche where the post office worker strolls into the building one day and kills, one by one, the people with whom he has worked for years.

Business and politics profess to be hardheaded, but how many businesses, and even countries, have been ruined through decisions that were ostensibly hardheaded but which had more to do with the reluctance of those in charge to face fears or vulnerabilities?

This reluctance to enter the deeper waters of the psyche is not confined to modern participants of corporate life. Fifteen hundred years ago in the Old English poem *Beowulf*, an anonymous bardic author confronted his listeners with a frightening image of this inner lake. His listeners were almost certainly rough warriors used to getting their hands dirty. He found them equally shy of that dark water.

DROPPING BENEATH THE SURFACE

Beowulf is a masculine story of descent into the waters of the unconscious, but where the restoration of a profound inner feminine power is essential to his survival. In that context it is a compelling story for both women and men working in a masculine workplace sorely in need of a commensurate balancing power. In a corporate culture still dominated by the image of the warrior archetype, Beowulf's plunge into the waters of the unconscious seems to be equally instructive for both sexes.

The early English teller of *Beowulf* asked his listeners to drop beneath the surface of their daily existence, where the rational mind continually prays for dry feet. Since that time the physical details of life may have changed. The elemental motifs have not. We could describe Beowulf himself as a sixth-century consultant. He was a prince and warrior who did not make his home in any one kingdom, but went offering his services to foreign kings for that same mixture of personal honor, self-education, prestige, and personal gain that motivates his modern consultative counterpart.

Hearing that Hrothgar, King of Denmark, was suffering the predations of Grendel, a diabolical swamp creature, he presented himself in Hrothgar's hall as the answer to his problems.

Apparently, at night, after the feasting and gift-giving was done, a large green creature smeared with mud would emerge from the lake, enter the hall, fight off Hrothgar's best warriors, tear men and women limb from limb, and drag their remains back to the swamp.

This image may seem outlandish to the modern mind, but it is a frighteningly accurate description of what happens to men or women who refuse to confront their more powerful creative urges. It is all very well in the broad light of day at work, or during the feasting and celebrations, when bonuses and employee-of-the-month wall plaques are being handed to the worthy; but at three in the morning, when we are alone, our defenses are down, and we cannot sleep, the huge green hand rises from below and drags us into something hitherto ignored, deeper and more urgent.

To the part of us that gets its sense of identity from the position it occupies in the hierarchy and the car it drives, it comes to feel as if it is being torn limb from limb. Most successful consultants and corporate trainers that I know, if they take the creative urgencies of their work seriously, wake up in strange hotel rooms at regular intervals and see familiar trails of blood leading back to this timeless swamp. Joseph Campbell used to say that if you do not come to know the deeper mythic resonances that make up your life, the mythic resonances will simply rise up and take you over. If you do not live out your place in the mythic pattern consciously, the myth will simply live *you* against your will.

Beowulf is welcomed by Hrothgar, and that night lies in wait for Grendel with his men inside Herot, Hrothgar's great hall. Sure enough, in the ensuing fight, Beowulf mortally wounds Grendel who then staggers back to die in the mere.

That night there is tremendous feasting and gift-giving. The problem, it seems, has been solved in one swift movement. But that night, as Beowulf sleeps with his men in a different hall, something *else* comes from the swamp to Herot, fights off the best warriors, and retreats with its human victim. Grendel's *mother*.

The message in this portion of the poem is unsparing. It is not the thing you fear that you must deal with, it is the *mother* of the thing you fear. The very thing that has given birth to the nightmare.

How many managers or consultants have solved the perceived difficulty in a place of work at the first stroke? Late one night the phone rings and the plant manager tells them that something else just arose from the depths of managerial discontent and is destroying the production and purpose they thought they had.

How many individuals have confronted a hard inner problem of their own, but in coming to a profounder understanding of its nature have discovered, standing behind it, something even more difficult to face?

The man who had been taken by Grendel's mother was the closest friend and confidant of Hrothgar. The king is grief-stricken. Visibly moved, Beowulf decides he must go down into the lake where Grendel's mother lives to confront her directly. The people are aghast that he would contemplate such a thing.

Beginning his description of the lake and sensing the tension of the moment, the anonymous bard telling the story says that no one knows where Grendel or his mother come from.

> *They named the huge one Grendel:*
> *If he had a father no one knew him,*
> *Or whether there'd been others before these two,*
> *Hidden evil before hidden evil.*

You can blame your mother, you can blame your father and *his* father for the problems with which you are destined to wrestle, but ultimately you are the one in whom they have made a home. You are the one who must say *Thus far and no farther*, and then go down and confront them yourself.

> *They live in secret places, windy*
> *Cliffs, wolf dens where water pours*
> *From the rocks, then runs underground, where mist*
> *Steams like black clouds,*

When the story tells us that they live in secret places, we are being told that Grendel's mother is the living incarnation of our disowned side, which has been forced to live in unfamiliar places, the fading-moon portion of ourselves, the part of us that refuses to show our limp, appearing in the bright light of our human social world for retribution.

The description of the frozen lakeshore reminds me of Kafka's statement *A good book should be an axe for the frozen sea within us.* This is a real description of the physical sensation of feeling blocked creatively and spiritually, and the wish to free the trapped waters of the human spirit. As we approach the edges of our creative comfort zone, the landscape appears more and more frozen. As if a spell has been cast over a cold land that spring can never visit. In the depression following the First World War, T. S. Eliot captured this blighted landscape of human numbness in his poem *The Waste Land.* A landscape where nothing seems to offer nourishment, nothing seems to fit, everything we see there lies, in Eliot's words, like "A heap of broken images." Traversing it, we stand literally petrified before the surface beneath which we must descend. At this point the storyteller offers a more disturbing detail:

> . . . *and the groves of trees*
> *Growing out over their lake are all covered*
> *With frozen spray, and wind down snake-like*
> *Roots that reach as far as the water*
> *And help keep it dark.*

Somehow the darkness of the lake is fed from above. What is above? The visible layers of consciousness are above. The personality. *We* are above. The implication is that the personality dwelling in the upper layers of consciousness is somehow feeding the interior darkness of the lake. We do not want to know what is down there, and we certainly do *not* want to know that the obscuring darkness is of our own making.

But the lake has a certain fiery quality to it despite its darkness.

> *At night that lake*
> *Burns like a torch. No one knows its bottom,*
> *No wisdom reaches such depths.*

This is to say that everyday human wisdom, the knowledge the personality depends on to corroborate its own existence, and the strategic methods upon which we have relied to get us to the edge will not suffice once we are beneath the surface. Something else is needed.

Then something appears at the lakeside, looking for refuge.

> *A deer,*
> *Hunted through the woods by packs of Hounds,*
> *A stag with great horns, though driven through*
> *   the forest*
> *From faraway places, prefers to die*
> *On those shores, refuses to save its life*
> *In that water.*

The news gets worse and worse. The strategic mind is useless but so also are our reserves of male courage. A deer, not only a deer, but that timeless image of maleness

> *a stag with great horns,*
> *. . . refuses to save its life*
> *In that water.*
> *. . . prefers to die*
> *On those shores,*

This portion of Beowulf is a magnificent translation by Burton Raffel. Here is the sequence, in full, describing the terrors of the lake:

> *They named the huge one Grendel:*
> *If he had a father no one knew him,*
> *Or whether there'd been others before these two,*
> *Hidden evil before hidden evil.*
> *They live in secret places, windy*
> *Cliffs, wolf dens where water pours*
> *From the rocks, then runs underground, where mist*
> *steams like black clouds, and the groves of trees*
> *Growing out over their lake are all covered*
> *With frozen spray, and wind down snake-like*
> *Roots that reach as far as the water*
> *And help keep it dark. At night that lake*
> *Burns like a torch. No one knows its bottom,*
> *No wisdom reaches such depths. A deer,*
> *Hunted through the woods by packs of Hounds,*
> *A stag with great horns, though driven through*
> > *the forest*

From faraway places, prefers to die
On those shores, refuses to save its life
In that water. It isn't far, nor is it
A pleasant spot!

When the storyteller says that "it isn't far," he knows we may be tempted to think this lake exists only in story, and, catching the listener, says, "Don't fool yourself; this very moment is the edge of the lake; this very intuition of possibility, the edge of our fear."

There are many ways in which we refuse, like the fearful stag, to save our life in that water. A friend of mine, Joel Henning, loves to recount the moment he preferred to die on that shore rather than enter the lake. Early on in his career, as he was first making his way as a consultant in the world, he was surprised to receive a call as if from on high, from his own equivalent of King Hrothgar in the form of George Armstrong, the president of the company he had been helping for some time. Joel was amazed and gratified that he would be called by the CEO personally. Could he come down to the office right away? Joel remembers dropping everything, including the meeting he was chairing at that very moment. As he left his office in Berkeley and sped across the Bay Bridge into San Francisco, he remembers how his hands gripped the steering wheel, thinking that here at last was his one chance to influence things in a substantial way. His possibility for an audience in the throne

room of the palace. His first real face-to-face with that
center of power and mystery, the chief executive of-
ficer.

As Joel entered the CEO's office directly from the
elevator on the top floor, he noticed immediately that
the entire office was white from floor to ceiling—
white furnishings, white curtains, and white floors.
Even the artwork was white. This royal aerie was in
fact a kind of mythical ice palace. In the far corner,
his desk at a forty-five-degree angle to Joel, sat the
man himself. The desk was placed below a backlit
alcove so that, as Joel says, George seemed to glow a
little, as if the recipient of some mysterious but continued benefaction.

The interview began with George royally thanking
Joel for all the good work he had done with the company. This thank-you was a little undermined by the
fact that George couldn't quite recall his loyal subject's name and insisted on calling Joel Jack. Joel
didn't correct him; that day Jack seemed fine to him;
he could live with it. Under these privileged circumstances why quibble over the small matter of his personal identity?

Then George got down to business. He realized
that Joel had become good friends with one of the
vice presidents, Robert. George wanted Robert to
take a job with the overseas division of the company.
Robert didn't want to go. "You know him, *Jack*, I'd
like you to take him aside and tell him that this move
is in his best interest."

Joel hesitated, recalling the standards of truth-telling and open, aboveboard honesty he had been recommending for the company to shake off its legacy of distrust. He put one toe in the dark water, saying, "You know, George, with all I've been recommending for the company, it might be better for you to tell Robert yourself." At that moment a large, hideous beast reared out of the lake. It said, using George as its fearsome mouthpiece, *"Jack,* I don't find that remark helpful for my purposes, *or* for your *future* with this company."

Joel hesitated for one moment more before this terrifying apparition, withdrew his foot from the water, and now, totally reincarnated as Jack, found that he suddenly agreed. All these years later, Joel says that the irrational vision that flashed before his eyes as he sat in the CEO's ice palace was of himself, his career totally finished because of the bad press from the sudden termination of this contract, wandering the streets of Berkeley as a bag lady. The fear was so palpable to Joel that, as if in a dream, the small matter of changing sex in order to become a bag *lady* was of little account. Whatever Joel's image of complete destitution was, he was sure to become it if he disagreed with George Armstrong.

In his training classes Joel stands before the participants as he gets to the moment of truth in the story and almost bellows, "What did I say to him, what did I say to George?"

"You told him you weren't going to compromise your ideals" "You refused," they call back.

"No, no, no," says Joel almost in triumph. "I said, George, *now* I understand what you wanted me to do. I'll talk to Robert over lunch, *today!*"

The point is, says Joel, that all of us at one time or another refuse that water. Not that this is an excuse for cowardice, but we must not think that only *other people* refuse to enter the darker side of their own psyche.

The harder point is that the fears are almost always irrational. You cannot reason them out of existence. If you could, they would have gone long ago. What does it take to have the maturity to admit the lake is there and then the deeper courage to slip beneath its still surface? To accept our own irrationality and the sober fact that we each bring it with us into the work-place and make far-reaching decisions based on ghostlike insecurities. Which begs another question: surely Beowulf possesses no immunity from insecurity, so what is it that enables this central character to go down into the lake?

To arm himself, Beowulf is given the helmet of the king, and a great and famous sword, Hrunting, but as the story makes clear, these do not help him except to bolster his courage in entering. At this point Beowulf's power seems to have more to do with a process of *disarming*.

The story of Beowulf makes it clear to us that although ordinary male courage and wisdom are indispensable, they are not enough to take us beneath the surface. We must possess something else. The story is very precise at this point. Of all the great Danish warriors and of all the flower of Saxon manhood who have accompanied Beowulf to Denmark, none of them can even contemplate descending into the depths of that water to wrestle with Grendel's mother. Only Beowulf has the quality that allows him to go down and confront her. I remember puzzling for a long time over the nature of this quality and its beckoning uncertainty. What does it take to go down there? I knew I had passed into her lair at crucial moments in my own life, but mostly as a swift and invisible visitor, not wanting to wrestle with her once I was there. One day, reading over Burton Raffel's translation of *Beowulf*, I found myself haunted by a memory of my own humiliation, years before in my mid-twenties.

STANDING AT THE EDGE

Standing at the very edge of that frightening cliff, I had decided to go back. The edge of this cold precipice seemed to mark the natural termination of my long trek. During a long month of bird-watching in the Nepalese Himalaya, I had been moving slowly up the Marsyandi river valley on the eastern side of the Annapurna range. I had parted from my two companions, a Belgian ornithologist and a Sherpa guide, telling them I needed a little time to myself, and then taking a parallel trail, I had promised to meet them farther up the valley in a few days.

On the afternoon of the second day, exhilarated by the clear, thin air and the ever-nearing white peaks rising around me, I turned sharply from an eroded cliff path high above an immense black gorge and found myself on a grassy shelf where the path turned from the rock wall and attempted to cross the drop.

I say attempted, because, to my utter dismay, the bridge itself was broken. The taut metal cables on one side of the narrow footbridge had snapped and the old rotted planks that made up its floor had concertined into a crazy jumble in the middle. Looking down through the gaps, I could see the dizzying three- or four-hundred-foot drop into the dark lichened gorge below.

I stopped right by the very entrance step to the bridge, calculated the movements I would have to make—a kind of entangled tightrope walk at full stretch between the two remaining cables on the left-hand side of the bridge—made as if to go, hestitated, then immediately retreated to a safely anchored sunlit rock to sit it out.

By now, after a month on the trail, time had telescoped. I had no phone calls to make, no deadlines to meet. I stared at the decrepit bridge for a long time, listening to the overwhelming but invisible rush of water in the black gash beneath me. I comforted myself that this was a long and honorable human tradition when confronted with an intractable problem. The hope is that the stare, if held long and hard enough, will cause the broken dream to spontaneously repair itself.

After an hour the bridge remained in its intractable state and I was equally intractable in refusing to cross it. This was a hard moment. I held to my heroic self-image tenaciously at this time in my youthful life. The nearest approximation to this self-glorified picture of myself would be the adventurous and indomitable spirit of Indiana Jones. In the late seventies, when I stood at the brink of that broken bridge, he was as yet a twinkle in George Lucas's eye, but I was soon to learn, ahead of his appearance on our screens, that a comic-book character can only be a mask for a human being wending his chaotic way to a modest maturity.

Though I was now on a cold grass ledge bewitched by the high white austerity of the Himalayas, I had only just left a close circle of young, immortal, and mostly male companions in some faraway Pacific islands. Working as naturalist guides for the Ecuadorian National Park Service in the Galápagos Islands, we had formed an association of heroes, a tight-knit group of young males who, despite our closeness, spent most of the time apart, aboard ship but essentially alone, guiding our visiting groups.

Depending on time, tide, and itinerary, we would at intervals congregate noisily in the bars of the islands' main harbor, Puerta Ayora. The focus of constant admiration from the polyglot international groups we shepherded, our arrogance and sense of immunity from the underbelly of human frailty was breathtaking. One or two even sported business cards inscribed with catchy titles such as "Blue Water Vagabond" or "Pacific Explorer." A very different life from the urban corporate work world, but essentially vulnerable to the same belief that God created the world simply in order to further our careers. Not the kind of life that deals easily with the portion of existence that continually pulls the rug, or, in this case, the bridge, from beneath carefully placed feet intent on a preordained path to stardom.

Besides this, I was not normally afraid of heights. A rock climber since my early teens, it seemed odd to be confronted with a sudden inexplicable attack of nerves. But since leaving Galápagos, traveling the Andes, and returning to Europe, I had felt something slowly tearing at the fabric of my perceptions. As I sat before the bridge, it was as if I faced a final and profound internal unraveling.

After an hour had passed, I had finally faced up to defeat, made an attempt to swallow my pride, and determined that there was nothing for it but to shoulder my pack and start back down the path. As I reached for my pack, I noticed the silhouette of a small but strangely shaped figure shuffling into view along the same cliff path that had brought me to the bridge. I saw her but she did not see me. An old bent woman, carrying an enormously wide-mouthed dung basket on her back, she saw nothing but the ground she was so intent on searching. In these bare high places, denuded of trees and fuel, yak dung dries quickly in the parched air and is harvested as a valuable fuel.

She shuffled, head bent, toward me, and seeing at last the two immense booted feet of a westerner, looked up in surprise. Her face wrinkled with humor as she registered her surprise, and in the greeting customary throughout Nepal, she bowed her head toward me with raised hands, saying, "*Namaste.*" The last syllable held like a song. "I greet the God in you."

I inclined my head and clasped my hands to reply, but before I could look up, she went straight across that shivering chaos of wood and broken steel in one movement. I saw her turn for a moment, smile almost mischievously, and then to my astonishment, she disappeared from the sunlight into the dripping darkness of the opposing cliff.

Incredulous, but without for one moment letting myself stop and think, I picked up my pack and went straight after her, crossing the broken bridge in seven or eight quick but frightening strides. Years later I wrote:

> *One day the hero*
> *sits down,*
> *afraid to take*
> *another step,*

and the old interior angel
limps slowly in
with her no-nonsense
compassion
and her old secret
and goes ahead.

"Namaste"
you say
and follow.

It seems to me that every man or woman comes to such a bridge at one time or another in their life, and we do not have to go on an adventure to the Himalaya to find it. Its equivalent happens every day in every glass and steel office structure across the country. Just the very moment we attempt to take a step in the right direction with a colleague, initiate a conversation, write a difficult memo, or take the first steps in a new direction, we can suddenly feel that the chasm is insurmountable and the bridge we had hoped to cross is down.

The broken bridge seems insurmountable because all our other demons rise to meet us at the prospect of a fall: visions of ourselves thrown onto the street; the future as a bag lady, envisioned so physically by Joel; or a sudden emptiness, a lack of confidence in our ability to do without all those many luxuries on which we have come to depend. In fact, as a presage of things to come, just as Beowulf and his entourage of warriors get to the water's edge, all kinds of smaller, slimy, scaly things writhe to the surface, horrifying everyone but Beowulf.

What are the modern corporate equivalents of these repressed monsters writhing just below the surface of our professional life? We can list a few of many. Most important: unresolved parent–child relationships that play out into rigid company hierarchies, paternal management systems, and dependent employees; unresolved emotional demands individuals may have of fellow workers but will never admit to themselves; the refusal to come to terms with an abused childhood; the subsequent longing for self-protection and the wielding of organizational power and control at any cost to gain that protection. Perhaps the parent of all these vulnerabilities is Beowulf's mother herself, the deep physical shame that we are not enough, will never be enough, and can never measure up.

Faced with these monsters, it seems that Beowulf is able to stop at the very edge of the lake and let the part of him represented by an older but wiser female energy go down with him, the part I met in the person of this wizened and diminutive Tibetan woman.

We are told that Beowulf goes down wearing ring mail, hard-forged steel rings woven into a protective suit. In the old mythology of sixth-century Middle Earth, the finest ring mail was forged by venerable trolls, and the strongest and most priceless by their *wives*. In mythological terms, this magical weaver is common to all cultures and appears as the Crone, the older woman who has given over the priorities of pleasing husband and family in order to pass on a tested and tightly knit feminine wisdom to the world. Ironically, hers is a stronger weave because she couples what Camille Paglia has called "the feminine mystery of self-impairment" to the outer revelations of male courage. She is the part of us that limps across the chasm when we cannot leap across. She is our vulnerability and our coming to terms with that vulnerability, and Beowulf refuses to go down into the lake without her. At some time in his life, Beowulf has learned self-compassion.

Clad in his web of rings, Beowulf leaps into the water and sinks to the very bottom of the lake, where Grendel's mother waits for him. There are clear, marvelous details etched into the story at this point. Beowulf finds that the great sword Hrunting, given to him by the Danes to help him in his pitch-black travail, is useless against this she-monster, as is another gift from above, the Danish king's helmet. He is forced to throw them away and wrestle barehanded with Grendel's mother. Locked together in a death-like embrace, they tumble into her den, where Beowulf sees, glowing on the wall, an unknown but marvelous sword. He breaks the chain on its hilt, and with a sudden blow, kills Grendel's mother with the glowing blade.

However well we arrange for our self-protection beforehand, our preparations are only muttered incantations to ward off the evil eye. The solution itself lies down in the water. The glamorous but useless sword given to Beowulf may also represent the attempt to rely inappropriately on technology at a crucial moment. Technology has marvelous benefits, as I can attest, sitting by my fireside, expanding this manuscript on my own personal talisman of the modern age, the laptop computer; but there are places where its writ does not run, for instance, in that split second of creative consciousness before the finger actually strikes the keyboard. In relationship to the fluid depths of the imagination it can only be a servant and not a master. Physically and metaphorically, my computer cannot go underwater, it is not built to withstand the turbulent and fathomless atmospheres of the soul.

Beowulf's friends wait all day at the very edge of the cold lake surface. The story says that he is down there for a very long time, to the point where he is given up for dead. The mythic code for "a very long time" is usually "three days and three nights." Jonah was three days and three nights in the belly of the whale; Gilgamesh was three days and three nights in the cave without food or water. Three days and three nights means an initiation, it means the process goes on longer than you would have it go on. Many scholars think it is connected to the moon's disappearance for three days each month, the darkest stretch of the heavenly cycle.

In the course of a human life we get to know these dark phases of existence quite well. Bereavement and rejection, loss of friends, family, and familiar way-signs. A person may go through the wrenching trauma of a divorce, which seems to stretch on for-ever, finally saying, "That is *it*, God, I've learned everything I need to know from this." But the trauma continues. An organization goes through radical re-structuring and those who work for it wonder when it will ever end. Three days and three nights. The temptation is not to follow through, to give up and go back to the old ways.

Whatever is needed for the moment of truth in those dire, deep places seems brought to view only on our arrival at the very bottom. So much of our experience is predicated on the consciousness with which we enter it, our future possibilities already mortgaged to past limitations. The struggling com-pany finds itself unable to see the chance of a more nimble future due to the suffocating weight of its past self-image. Beowulf's final struggle and grasping of the luminous sword must be seen as the vital and nec-essary ability to shift shapes at the crucial moment and grasp the opportunity offered. Traditionally rehearsed speeches fail to win agreements during dif-ficult negotiations. The prepared speeches, talis-manically, like Hrunting, may take you down, into the thick of it, to the monster that lies between you and the other side, but once there, you must rely on the gritty truth you pluck from the very walls of the meeting room to bring the wrestling to a conclusion.

KILLING GRENDEL'S MOTHER

Fairy stories and myths are full of creatures and people that at one time or another kill or are killed. Beowulf kills Grendel's mother, and the story does not attempt to soften this fact. Young children seem to know instinctively at this point that something marvelous and terrible has happened. As I read to my seven-year-old son, he stops the proceedings. Immediately, he wants to know why the monster was killed, who killed it, and, being a boy, what particular weapon was used. There is a felt sense that a threshold has been passed beyond the mere love of gory detail. My instinct is to say that the killing of Grendel's mother has as much to do with a particular depth of integration as it has to do with the severing it so well describes. Carnivore or vegetarian, we live at the center of a profound web of killing and enjoy its manifestations every time we open a refrigerator door or pull on a pair of leather boots. We are dependent on the eating and dismemberment of many other creatures and have been so since our evolutionary appearance in the shape of the first hominid. This knowledge is deeply embedded in the way we view our experience of the world, though it is rarely faced and admitted.

If we take recent human evolution as our perspective, modern men and women are emerging only now from the mythological constructs of the hunter-gatherer. The time of the human family's Great Hunt stretched for hundreds of thousands of years and reached its peak with the emergence of Homo sapiens as a distinctive human species about one hundred thousand years ago.

All the developments we most closely associate with human endeavor—farming, cities, enormous population growth, and the control and molding of nature—have occurred in the transparent, wafer-thin period of the last ten thousand years. The office environment is barely a few centuries old, and in the electronic form we encounter it, one generation old. Little wonder that as hunter and gatherer under the endless skies of the savannah, the human spirit should be struggling to adapt to this dizzying change in our outward circumstances, and that old motifs and stories such as *Beowulf*, reaching back far earlier than its sixth-century composition, still hold the key to many of our difficulties.

If we look at the thought and feeling that we have inherited from the time of our long hunter-gatherer evolution, we can see a pattern to this fascination with death in our fairy stories, myths, and movies. Preparations for the hunt have been remarkably consistent through time, and among different cultures, right down to the surviving hunter-gatherer peoples of today. One of the tribe would dress himself in the pelt or feathers of the animal to be hunted. The ensuing dance would be an imitation of the hunt to come, culminating in the pretended ritual killing of the masked human being.

One interpretation has been that by simply enacting this ritual we believed we could bring about a better possibility for a successful hunt. A more imaginative view might be that in a time when the veil was very thin between human beings and the world we inhabited, the ritual was a continual reminder that we were stalking a part of ourselves. That to enter fully into the sacramental act we had to become the animal itself and realize fully that in taking from our world, we were in fact killing a part of ourselves. In a sense we *become* the animal that is killed, as it becomes a part of us when it is eaten.

In a myth, fairy story, or legend, the act of killing is a signal that, in effect, a deeper kind of integration has occurred. What do we mean by integration at this stage in the story?

When the story announces that Beowulf has *killed* Grendel, we are being told that Beowulf has *become* Grendel, and that when he *kills* Grendel's mother, he has *become* Grendel's mother. He has wrestled with his interior and exterior monsters to the point where he admits them as himself. The successful careerist may find that the darkness embroiled at his center is the part that *wishes* to fail in order to open other neglected parts of his life; when he *becomes* his failure he no longer has to carry that career success as a burden. He can explore avenues that he previously might have labeled under that dreaded American swamp-dwelling monster *failure*.

Dramatically, Beowulf rises to the surface with the severed head of Grendel, whose body he found after searching the den. But the sword that Beowulf found and then used to such great effect in the depths of the lake has melted and dissolved away in Grendel's blood. A mesmerizing image. This is a clear way of saying that as the enemy that has frightened us melts away, so does the requisite need for the weapon of attack, simply because human nature being what it is, this inner arms procurement industry eventually becomes a law unto itself, ingratiating itself within the personality as a defense against life itself, like an enormous, overbudgeted inner Pentagon, institutionalized, literally, into the life of the body politic.

In *Songs of Experience*, Blake wrote of his guardian angel attempting to visit him while Blake fought him off, mistaking him for just another aspect of that wider world he had already turned into an enemy.

> *So he took his wings and fled;*
> *Then the morn blushed rosy red;*
> *I dried my tears and armed my fears*
> *With ten thousand shields and spears.*
>
> *Soon my angel came again:*
> *I was arm'd, he came in vain;*
> *For the time of youth was fled*
> *And grey hairs were on my head.*

The second aspect of the dissolving sword reminds us that we can never ultimately show to others exactly *how* we slew the monster. Like Beowulf, we rise from the lake with the severed head but look down to find only the hilt of the sword we used, good now only to be thrown away.

Don't, says the story, get carried away with your display of inner mastery and try to wield that same inner sword in the world above. Your delusions of grandiosity will melt away as soon as you try to use it again. What is real and useful in the inner world does not necessarily translate immediately into the world to which you return. It takes some skill and not a little patience to find how much you have really changed, and what of your new world view will work.

This kind of discrimination seems to be crucial in the integration of the fluid creative world of the inner psyche with the outer empirical world of the tried and true. The lack of distinction around these two has caused many a hardheaded organization to shy away from explorations of emotional and spiritual well-being, for fear of these subterranean psychic swords being wielded aboveground in the small confines of the office cubicle. Stepping into the wilder depths of the unconscious and feeling the exhilaration of those subterranean currents can be exciting, but it can be sobering to realize the equivalent depth of discrimination that is demanded in order to recognize the many different levels of the psyche and the action that is appropriate to each of them.

In the contemplative traditions there have always been refreshing checks and balances on the grandiosity of the ego as it smells the possibility for power during spiritual exploration. In the Zen tradition, for instance, although students were asked to involve themselves in long periods of inner intensity and silence, they were also asked to continually test their silent inner states against the concreteness of the outer world, and to know the distinction between the two.

A famous Zen master, while weighing flax on a scale, was once asked the meaning of Zen by a student. Without taking his concentrated eyes off the scale, he adjusted the weights and said, "Three pounds of flax."

St. John of the Cross, alone in his room in profound prayer, experienced a rapturous vision of Mary. At the same moment he heard a beggar rattling at his door for alms. He wrenched himself away and saw to the beggar's needs. When he returned, the vision returned again, saying that at the very moment he had heard the door rattle on its hinges, his soul had hung in perilous balance. Had he not gone to the beggar's aid, she could never have appeared to him again.

The confusion is difficult to deal with. There is an old saying in the Zen Buddhist tradition: "Before Zen study, mountains are mountains, and rivers are rivers; during Zen study, mountains are no longer mountains and rivers are no longer rivers; after Zen study,

mountains are mountains again and rivers are rivers."
Of course, this all sounds very linear: before, during,
and after, with enlightenment coming comfortably at
the end; but essentially, all three states are usually
experienced in one fell swoop, which is why Grendel *wrestles*.

DISCLOSURE AND VULNERABILITY

The internal willingness to wrestle with our inner
demons does not necessarily mean that anyone else
in the office is brought into the drama. The real
achievement is found when we acknowledge that
these unresolved forces, our demons, affect our lives
and those who work with us tremendously, simply because everything we do is determined by the fears and
hopes we bring to a situation. Recognizing the presence of these forces in our own outlook, we can stop
them from playing out unconsciously with our colleagues in the workplace. Nevertheless, a form of
healing seems to take place when we find a truly sym-
pathetic ear for our more difficult struggles. Just the
opposite occurs when we confide in someone who is
simply not interested or is secretly scared to death of
what we have just revealed.

Goethe begins a famous German poem with the
admonition

Tell a wise person or else keep silent.

Our deeper struggles are in effect our greatest spiritual and creative assets and the doors to whatever creativity we might possess. It seems to be a learned wisdom to share them with others only when they have the possibility of meeting them with some maturity. We learn to remain attentive to the mood and outlook of the listener even before we begin to speak about the darker side of our existence.

Are they really listening? Do they really want to know? Is this frightening them? Will they think I am so weak that it will affect our work relationship for the worse? This last worry is usually connected to something in ourselves. Do we have *confidence* in our struggles? Are they really our own, or are they another's struggle that we have simply borrowed in order to postpone a personal inner confrontation?

A mature individual should be able to handle any struggle we have confided in him. But many times the telling of such stories may overwhelm the listener. He may be paying close attention to our tale of woe, but cannot tell his own fears from the fears he is hearing from another's mouth. In a way, he is made uncomfortably aware of his own dark areas without having developed the skills to explore it himself. Our story, in effect, becomes a kind of persecution, as if the listeners are being pushed through a door they are not yet ready to enter. This feeling of persecution may lead to a kind of knee-jerk cutting comment or evasion on their part. Taking their comment as an attack rather than the desperate defense it is, we may feel devastated by their reaction. If we are paying enough attention at the beginning, we can stop our self-revelation before we scare them to death and elicit a fight-or-flight reaction. We could see this ability to really listen as a litmus test of those mythical creatures, the "empowered" and "unempowered" manager.

The *empowered* manager might be one who has some understanding of his or her own dark side and inner struggles. When she sees the possibilities for failure in those she manages, *she does not mistake them as her own*. She can give them some room and understanding, she can allow others to experiment and sometimes fail. There are also those who cannot come to terms with the cyclical up-and-down nature of human experience; they have an irrational need to be eternally competent and expect others to be the same. A period of disclosure to such a person during a particularly difficult time can lead to the confessor being seen as thoroughly and eternally weak, an image that may be difficult to shake.

Finally, is it possible to keep on *working* while we grapple with the worry? There is something real about this question, beyond the puritanical finger-wagging of the work ethic. The answer is often yes. Work itself can continue to serve as a reference point, a grounding anchor point, outside of the necessarily chaotic reformation which is occurring in the psyche. *Psyche* herself, personified in Greek myth as a

quintessential representative of the awakening feminine, was set to work by Aphrodite in this fashion,
counting and sorting seeds, this fine, detailed work
serving as the greater metaphor of our lives, finding
and recognizing what belongs together.

All in all, taking the above into account, we might
wonder why we ever open our mouths at all! It may
be in fact that there is no other listening ear in the
workplace and the outer parts of the struggle are accomplished with family, friends, or the stranger who
opens up a conversation on the flight to Cincinnati.
In Europe there is a long tradition of telling, during
long train journeys, one's whole life story to complete
strangers. It allows the heart to ruminate on matters
we are fearful of broaching in the company of those
it may concern.

DISAPPEARANCE AND RETURN

A close friend of mine, a senior manager for a large
London publishing company and the epitome of
steadiness and understatement, suddenly, around
thirty-five, found himself plunged into a complete
abyss over the path his life had taken. He looked
around one day and wondered how he could carefully
construct, over so many years, a daily life he could
barely endure.

In a catastrophically short time he came to the

edge of a nervous breakdown. The state of his soul became imperative to him, but his very professionalism at work prevented him from giving himself the time to wrestle with the long-buried compulsions and neglected longings that to his distress were now rising to the surface of his consciousness. In an act of courage he asked for an open-ended leave from the company to deal with his emotional life. In an equal act of courage, the company gave it to him. He was told to take the time he needed.

The next few months of the fall were spent with family and friends, taking a hard look at the way his life was constellated. Everything was up for appraisal, including the place of his work. Toward the end of his two-month sabbatical from work, I made a sudden decision to fly to Britain and join him. We took off for the Welsh borderlands, exploring the mist-wreathed hills of that frosty December, fetching up in small pubs and inns, continually picking up the conversation around old threads of his life and possible new directions.

We reached the bottom of Grendel's lake in the small Shropshire town of Church Stretton, sheltering from the freezing damp in a small café. After three days of being the eternally supportive friend, I took a deep breath and said something about him I knew he wouldn't like. Almost immediately our conversation turned adversarial. I briefly remember making some wild statement, almost like an accusation, an appraisal of one portion of his life about which only a close friend could have the arrogance or foolishness to make. I can't remember the details, only the absurd but eternally English background noises of tea being poured into china mugs. Fixing him with my best steely glare, I told him something about the way he was, and that he shouldn't *be* the way he was, that I was disappointed in him, and that he had better change or he would never surface again.

Looking back, it wasn't even important whether I was right or not, only that I felt his will re-engage half in outrage and half in recognition of what I had said. He first went white and silent, slowly warmed into a violent pink, and in best English fashion strode off to make a phone call to his wife. "Well done, David," I said to myself, "with friends like me, who needs enemies?" But when he returned and sat down again, I felt in a strange way that he had met, recognized, and now accepted something of himself he had only half known previously as monstrous. Like Grendel, it had until now been a raider on his sanity, an interloper and violator of the grand hall of his upper conscious mind.

If the event had mythological overtones, the weather conspired, as it should so close to the Celtic borderlands, in appropriate fashion. Taking a winding single-track road of impossible steepness out of the village, we emerged from that bone-numbing mist on the roof of a new world. Beneath us lay a landscape of white arctic mist as far as the eye could see, here and there revealing the dark bodies of half-hidden hills. The straw-colored uplands were burnished by bright winter sunshine to a warm gold, flecked with green from the bracken.

We spent the afternoon-long walk mostly in silence, exhilarated by the cold air and clear skies, finishing on a serene valley road bordered by fields and farms, along which for over an hour, unaccountably, no car or truck came to disturb our peace.

Looking back, that afternoon became the pivot around which the compass needle of my friend's future life began to move. The crisis was not simply about his work life, nor was it his home life alone. When the soul begins to turn over and prepare its internal ground for the new season, it refuses to make those distinctions so easily.

The point is that we eventually come to the realization that it is injurious to the soul to remove portions of our life from exploration, as if, at work, certain parts of experience suddenly lie out of bounds. We simply spend too much time and have too much psychic and emotional energy invested in the workplace for us to declare it a spiritual desert bereft of life-giving water.

The belief has been that we can drink only on weekends or vacations and must proceed to shrivel slowly as the desiccating years roll by. Whatever strategy we employ, or whoever we choose to speak with, we are eventually compelled to bring our work life into the realm of spiritual examination. Life does not seem to be impressed by our arguments that we can ignore our deeper desires simply because we happen to be earning a living at the time.

If the first steps along the creative path almost always involve awaking in Dante's dark wood, or descending down to meet Grendel's mother, then a narrow image of what it means to be professional can continually prohibit us from taking *any* first step as we vainly attempt to exclude human darkness and inner struggle from work life. What would it be like to take a professional approach to the longings of our soul for fulfillment in the world?

Whatever seemingly small possibilities we have for including our struggles in our work life, there seems little choice but to look for them. Whether we work with supportive or unsupportive colleagues, we will always be hunted by what we have most denied in ourselves. Waking or sleeping, it takes many different forms, but most often the shape of a devouring creature trying to include us, literally, in the greater body of its experience. If outer corporate inertia is used as an excuse for our own hesitations, we become the frightened stag at the edge of the lake, looking back to find that our deeper longings have turned, suddenly, to the snarling teeth of pursuing hounds.

Ironically, our place of refuge is the lake where the greater devouring animal of our disowned desire lies in the shape of Beowulf's mother. The refusal to go down into the lake is the refusal to be eaten by life. The delusion is that there might be a possibility of immunity from the natural failures that accompany the soul's explorations in the world. But the story says you are going to be swallowed by something greater one way or another. The question is whether you will give yourself to that greater life consciously.

The German poet Rilke said:

> *Winning does not tempt that man.*
> *This is how he grows: by being defeated, decisively*
> *by constantly greater beings.*

The only real question is not one of winning or losing, but of experiencing life with an ever-increasing depth. The storyteller says, why not go down, at home or at work, into the lake, consciously, like Beowulf. Don't die on the shore. The stakes are very high; the stakes are your life.

Fire in the Earth

Earth

Toward a Grounded Creativity

73
▼

The luminous sword that Beowulf snatches in the depths of his interior struggle is like a point of light concentrated from the fiery depths into which he has let himself fall. This is a marvelous image of our struggles for the merest touch of creativity in the workplace. Out of the maelstrom of events and the ever-changing patterns around us we take hold of something small, sharp, and substantial, and down in the depths, hidden from others, change our existence in the light-filled world above.

Out of the shifting nature of the workplace, out of a hundred details, a dozen conversations, a trip into the field, a pile of reports, a screen full of figures, we pluck, like Beowulf, the one concentrated point of the pattern from which we can act. This process is at the heart of poetic inspiration and the poetic imagination; it gives equal place to the tiny act as the greater pattern and demands that we stop choosing between the small actions that make up the everyday and the great sweeps of the larger plan and take time to know a world where each has its place. It is exactly the kind of skill that is needed in the overheated corporate world now emerging around us, not only because the ability to stretch between these two fiery and opposing poles will help us survive as businesspeople, but because it offers the distinct possibility of a work life we might actually want for ourselves.

Understanding the fiery moments hidden within the daily round of work, we come to understand a contradictory part of our nature—our love of creative fire, its warmth and its intensity, and at the same time our fear of being burnt. What opportunities and fears do we face while attempting to be more passionate and creative in a workplace that may seem hostile to our intentions? It is a call in effect to fight fire with another kind of fire, one that poets of all epochs have attempted to uncover at the very center of our nature.

FIRE AND DESIRE

Fire is an abiding image of our time. The word *hot* is used instinctively now for what is current, compelling, exciting, or sexually alluring. But there is also a deeper experience of fire smoldering inside human beings independent of what is fleeting and fashionable. Fire has been the touchstone of human creativity and passion since the beginning of our literate and aural history. At work or at home we are *fired* by enthusiasm, *branded* with cowardice, and *inflamed* with sexual desire. We find ourselves in the *heat* of the moment, or *burned* by circumstances. We look for the creative *spark*, long for human *warmth*, and in times of need, call on the *fire* in our bellies. And bereft of these, we are left with only *ashes*.

But we are equally wary of other qualities of fire and passion, the flashy deal maker who looks good in the moment yet leaves everyone saddled with debt: the violence of stifled passion let loose on coworkers, the hot razzmatazz of certain advertising that inveigles people to buy through false images and seductive sound. Fire and passion have always been a two-edged sword. Yet if we do give up our personal desires and passions hoping to get above it all, we almost always find ourselves substituting the passions and desires of someone more charismatic for our own, and wake up later to find ourselves in their thrall.

Being in touch with fire and passion seems to be an essential need for the soul of a human being. Yet in our suspicion of those desires that lead to selfishness and self-indulgence we often throw out those more essential desires that have to do with our creativity and personal destiny.

One of the distinguishing features of corporate America until recently was its demand that the individual give up those personal desires which could not be met materially by the corporation. "Sacrifice now for future unstated promises" was how consultant Peter Block phrased that old call to loyalty in his book *The Empowered Manager*. This kind of loyalty is no longer required. In some ways it was always something of an illusion, but with large corporations shedding jobs continually over the past decade, it has increasingly come to mean less and less. It is the smaller or newer companies, needing tighter, more creative teams of people to whom less and less is promised outside of their present creative engagements that have set the tone for the years to come. As John Sculley, formerly of Apple Computer, said: "The new corporate contract is that we'll offer you an opportunity to express yourself and grow, if you promise to leash yourself to our dream, at least for a while."

There is something at once disturbing and realistic about this statement. If we are going to leash ourselves to others' dreams, we had better make sure they are congruent or compatible with our own. If they are not, then we may be simply enrolling ourselves in a system bent to the desires of others. John Sculley knows where he is going; we celebrate his clarity. But his statement is a call to a greater watchfulness; we ourselves had better know where we are going, too, or we might become slaves to the desires and needs of someone else's destiny, which for all its qualities has nothing to do with our own path. When the contract does come to an end, we may be left with a lingering bad taste that causes us to wrestle with self-worth and self-esteem when we could just as well be wrestling with our next engagement.

Loyalty in an organization is now based on two ends of the creative spectrum—security in the form of money, power, and benefits; and creative engagement by way of excitement and innovation. The balance point on the scale between security and creativity is very different for each of us, but whatever our personal balance point, there is no doubt that the postmodern corporation is demanding more movement and adaptation to the insecure and mutable end of experience. It wants vitality and fire, not because it likes the dangerous beauty of these qualities, but because it will not survive without them. The hard news is that the corporate world wants us around while we are useful, but it offers no security based on how likable or impassioned we are.

The individuals working in this alchemical environment are continually forced to reassess their abilities to live with unknown and open-ended situations, to actively create their own life independent of the organization and to *like themselves* while they are doing it.

But the corporation must understand that this adaptation on the part of an individual comes as a gift from the soul. A soulful approach to work is probably the only way an individual can respond creatively to the high-temperature stress of modern work life without burning to a crisp in the heat. It takes the soul's ability to elicit texture, color, story, and meaning from the tumult of events, to meet fire with fire and still have a somewhat restful existence that is capable of wise policy somewhere at the center of it all. The corporation, in calling for a little more creative fire from their people, must make room for a little more soul. Making room for creativity, it must make room for the source of that fire and the hearth where it burns—the heart and the soul of the individual.

By understanding this essential and ancient relationship of creativity and fire, and attempting to speak from and live with the flame of personal passion, there is a possibility of understanding how difficult yet how magnificent the creative path of any individual can be, even within the confines of an organization.

To some extent, while we think we are simply driving to work every morning to earn a living, the soul knows it is secretly engaged in a life-or-death struggle for its existence. As a nation we have chosen to invest enormous amounts of our time and energy in the corporate American workplace, so much time and energy, in fact, that the soul is often forced to choose our work environment, even if it is measured by the short length of a desk, as the place it will make or break its way to the surface of our existence or "die" in the attempt. No matter how confined, to the soul everything is at stake, and everything in the flame of that existence is to be lost or won.

FIRE AND ICE

Early in our evolution and long before the corporate office began to form in the human imagination, we were awed and terrified by the fire that issued from the rocks and smoldering cones around us. Our earliest communities were also born around the blackened fire circles now being found in the soils of East Africa.

Those circles of fire were the pivot around which our storytelling and language began. We must have listened to the first stories over the crack of twigs, with our faces warmed by the fire's heat and our backs chilled by the surrounding dark. Little wonder that fire lies at the center of what we understand to be alive and engaged. Yet being so close to the fire, we must have many times turned our heads toward that outer darkness, made all the darker and more frightening in contrast to the heat and light that warmed us.

Our small blaze was not only the center of a private world, then, but the central light about which pivoted a vast and terrible unknown. Being unable to live at the center of light or out in the blackness itself, we were always at the periphery of two worlds—light and dark, heat and cold, fire and ice.

Perhaps through fire we also inherit an intuitive memory of the beginning of time itself, an old image reminding us that we are literally sparks struck from the flint of creation itself, descendants of that impossible fireball that scientists assure us started everything going. Gazing into that imagined flame before our eyes we intuit the full spectrum of human experience in one mesmerizing dance. As an image, fire seems to lie at the center of human life, whether we are hunched over our desks scribbling down notes for a spark of inspiration or breathing life into a few embers in the wilderness. We wonder at its power to transfix and draw us in, and at the same time to hold us at a distance from its very center.

Fire holds two qualities simultaneously. Firstly, it is a source of tremendous nourishment. To this day, no matter our technology, we still look to the soulful qualities of fire to warm our hands, sear our summer meals at the barbecue, and fill our winters with the flicker of its light. If we can, we give it the place of honor at the very center of our home and hearths.

When we try for something a little more fiery and creative in our work, even in the air-conditioned comfort of a sixth-floor office, we are moving toward the ancient mythic and molten abodes of metalwork, sacrifice, and alchemy: a place where we give up at least as much as we are given. In almost all cultures and religions, fire carries not only the heat of primordial creation but the dance of energy that devours and sublimates the outworn. Warming our hands we feel its benefit; stand too close and we must submit to its alchemical effect on the soul and the senses. It not only warms the household of identity (in modern language, makes us feel good about ourselves), but burns our house to the ground (brings on a crisis of identity), takes everything we own and turns us out, without rhyme or reason, into the new but unknown life we must call our own.

One way to avoid this is to take the path of ice, to

freeze everything and everyone around us so that they cannot move or take light. The Victorian father took the path of ice, waving his cold wand over anything combustible in the household—children, wives, servants. Modern corporations until now have done much the same, taking on the role of the parent who cools and secures everything, but in doing so, rimes everything it has touched with bureaucratic hoarfrost.

But each of us contains an icy sliver of that parental figure. For safety's sake, we all take the path of ice at one time or another in order to cool the passion of events, but most especially in the workplace, simply because we stand to lose so much in any conflagration; if our creative approach goes wrong, such things as power, money, relationship, and the respect of our peers are all at stake. The higher the stakes, the more likely we are to turn to the cooling abilities of ice to save us. Do it as a habit and we find ourselves like the Bronze Age man recently discovered entombed in an alpine glacier, preserved for generations to come, but dead to the present in which we are found.

Fire and ice are timeless images appearing again and again in the poet's mind. The poets of Elizabethan England in particular were hypnotized by these two sides of experience, as if recreating their nation's simultaneous exploration of Africa and the Arctic. In the corporation today we must make a timeless home between the fierce heat of innovation and the cool winds of consolidation.

We live, it seems, no matter our time, between two fires, one hot and one cold, and because real creativity has always had an undercurrent of death and resurrection to it, as poets or managers we must intuitively wonder in which element we are to eventually perish. Here is Robert Frost, earlier this century, in his intimate but understated New England voice, mulling the possibilities.

FIRE AND ICE

Some say the world will end in fire
Some say in ice.
From what I've tasted of desire
I hold with those who favor fire.
But if it had to perish twice,
I think I know enough of hate
To say that for destruction ice
Is also great
And would suffice.

This familiar knife edge between nourishment and terror, between everything that is passionate and everything that is numb with cold, seems to lie, like the fire warming our hearts, at the center of human aspiration. Our own fiery possibilities for a passionate and creative life carry with them at all times the possibility of being burnt by failure or cast into the outer darkness of frustration. Asked to speak a creative but disturbing truth and we freeze at the prospect and hold our tongue. Better, we might think, to keep that fire hidden, a chilled destiny lived out on the level of frustration far preferable to a fulfillment that burns out before our eyes, and worse perhaps at work, before other's eyes. We never step fully into the darkness, but neither do we step toward the flame of our most central belonging and become the fire itself.

The fear that our flaws may be revealed to others or that we may lose the work relationships which sustain us through risky creative action and the burning away of surface appearances has been one of the timeless underlying themes of poetry and drama, themes which still inform our everyday attempts to live out the soul's desires at work.

Take any step toward our destiny through creative action (it may be as simple as lifting a pen over a blank sheet of paper), and we know intuitively that we are giving up whatever cover we had. Tiptoeing like the unwitting souls of classical myth who blundered into Pan on the mountainside, we have ventured into the sacred temenos of our own desiring and startled a god. The universe turns toward us, realizing we are here, alive and about to make our mark. We hear the wild divine elements in the world hold their breath, waiting for our next move, our next word, but at last the center of real attention, we turn quietly and take a step back, into the shadow of the trees, and, hopefully, a quieter life.

Having backed away from the moment, we try hard not be found. We hope we can remain quiet and not be found. We know through long experience that having followed our personal passions, we not only warmed ourselves around that flame but were drawn mesmerically to the possibility of total failure at its center. A center that holds the promise of a new life but seems to be ready to burn up most of our present life to achieve it.

We hope that this double-edged nature of reality can't be true; no one told us it would lead to this. At this point in the creative process we engage in an internal dialogue of disbelief. The hope is to stay in the background away from the fire, and wait for someone or something to come along and grant us immunity from these difficulties and sacrifices, someone to offer reassurance, saying perhaps, "Take the safe way, not the way of passion and creativity, as the path to your destiny, to the life you desire. Follow it and you can never be touched. I will take care of you *completely,* all along the way." This false reassurance may be heard in the form of an inner voice or it may be what the parental figure of the corporation continually assures us by its all encompassing father-mother presence and its payment of our medical benefits.

We can't underestimate the draw of this parental reassurance. I remember, along with my wife, feeling tremendous pangs of loss around resigning our positions from an American international school whose courses we directed in England. Though our salaries were not exceptional, they provided all our living expenses, travel between the United States and England for our twice-yearly get-togethers, and a ready-made family made up of our fellow directors from countries around the world. My creative destiny as prospective poet yanked and pulled at me to return to the States, but the long months of disentanglement from that emotional mother-father matrix were extremely painful.

THE PATH OF FIRE

In my experience, the more true we are to our own creative gifts the less there is any outer reassurance or help at the beginning. The more we are on the path, the deeper the silence in the first stages of the process. Following our path is in effect a kind of going *off* the path, through open country. there is a certain early stage when we are left to camp out in the wilderness, alone, with few supporting voices. Out there in the silence we must build a hearth, gather the twigs, and strike the flint for the fire ourselves.

This can be a frightening time. Faced with the silence that we meet in our first steps, we may turn pale and quiet ourselves. There are wild and, we suspect, dangerous animals living in the wilderness we have entered, animals we might not be so frightened of, or think so much about, if we were out there with someone else. In the silence these animals make sudden and frightening cries, in their roars can be heard distinctly familiar words: *mortgage, car payments, health insurance.* Hearing them, we may drop out of sight and lie low, hoping they won't find us and devour us alive.

Faced with these fears in the corporate wilderness, the strategist and designer inside us begins to work on new and subtle forms of invisibility, perhaps sinking into the cover offered by the organization. Not being engaged by the forceful nature of our own personal creativity, we may give ourselves to our fears more easily and so seek safety through preemptive attacks on others. We may seek out those who have power already, and bind ourselves to their desires in exchange for their protection. If we do not find that shelter, then for safety's sake we may begin to develop an advanced form of stealth technology; we learn to lower our profile as we fly through the day to make sure no one can find us. As with the designer of a modern jet fighter, the hope may be to get our radar profile down to such an extent that we no longer show up on an organization's radar screen. As Garry Trudeau put it: "I am trying to cultivate a life-style that does not require my presence." A moment of comic relief from Mr. Trudeau, but one that admits that we are continually hiding our light under a bushel because we feel safer that way.

At the beginning of a radically creative decision, then, we may hear an interior voice guaranteeing us complete safety if we take a particular route. Hearing that smooth reassurance, we have to know that this is the strategic part of the mind speaking. A useful portion of consciousness, but used alone, a part of us unequipped for living in the pathless lands we have opened by our willingness to move in new, unsignposted directions.

In effect, if we can see the path ahead laid out for us, there is a good chance it is not our path; it is probably someone else's we have substituted for our own. Our own path must be deciphered every step of the way. There is surely a place for the strategic mind, the ability to plan, that lays out our every step in advance, but its ability to pay the monthly bills and figure out the social security tax can become an end in itself. What would it be like to link these powers of calculation and strategy with a radical embrace of the creative unknown, to put strategy in the service of soul?

The soul says something more radical and frightening to us, wholly unlike the soothing reassurances of the strategic mind. Out of the silence the soul startles us by telling us *we are safe already*, safe in our own experience, even if that may be the path of failure. Soul loves the journey itself. The textures and undulations of the path it has *made* through the landscape by hazard and design, are nourishing in themselves. I can recall many long wilderness treks myself, where the difficulties and desperations of being in rough country have slowly, over the days, quieted the internal dialogue to a mute whisper. A river becomes a river, not a river barring my way.

Entering the river, it becomes a *cold* river; the reluctance to experience bracing cold is revealed as the obstacle, and not the river itself. If we are stopped and experience a few hellish moments of desperation, then in retrospect we find ourselves remembering the vitality and aliveness of those times. They become as precious to the memory as the days of uninterrupted walking. The soul, in knitting together experience out of the events of our lives, to our bafflement and distress, is as protective of its trials and failures as its personal victories.

THE CENTER OF THE FLAME

I was once out in a fearful storm, kayaking in the Pacific Northwest, far from land and terribly frightened. Caught on those huge shoulders of water lifting me torward the sky, after many hours I finally broke through the spray and my own terror to an experience of pure vitality. I was uncovering a quality inside me that had been stifled for years through my refusal to wake up to things just as they were. But the storm, and the real possibility of drowning, opened up an instinctual response inside me; my body and the double-bladed paddle became one organism, and I somehow found a path to the shore through those waves that belonged to the sea's fury and rhythm and also, at the same time, were peculiarly my own.

Recalling the experience afterward in a poem called *Out on the Ocean*, I wrote the following lines:

> *the blades flash*
> *lifting veils of spray as the bow rears*
> *terrified then falls*
>
> *with five miles to go*
> *of open ocean*
> *the eyes pierce the horizon*
>
> *the kayak pulls round*
> *like a pony held by unseen reins*
> *shying out of the ocean*
>
> *and the spark behind fear*
> *recognized as life*
> *leaps into flame*
>
> *

> *Always this energy smoulders inside*
> *when it remains unlit*
> *the body fills with dense smoke.*

The last lines came as a shock. A reminder that refusing to open to the fire and vitality in our nature, whether it be out on the ocean or riding the crest of a stormy meeting room is not a passive process. We cannot neglect our interior fire without damaging ourselves in the process. A certain vitality smolders inside us irrespective of whether it has an outlet or not. *When it remains unlit, the body fills with dense smoke.* I think we all live with the hope that we can put off our creative imperatives until a later time and not be any the worse for it. But refusing to give room to the fire, our bodies fill with an acrid smoke, as if we had covered the flame and starved it of oxygen. The interior of the body becomes numbed and choked with particulate matter. The toxic components of the smoke are resentment, blame, complaint, self-justification, and martyrdom.

The longer we neglect the fire, the more we are overcome by the smoke. But at least we have the comfort of remembering the old saying No smoke without fire. If we are suffering the consequences of asphyxiation from the smoldering fuel inside us, we are at least aware there is a fire and fuel there to find and breathe on.

EMBRACING GRIEF AND JOY

Images of magnificent storms and the wilderness of the Pacific Northwest may seem far from our workday in the office, but holding two contrasting images may serve to our advantage as we ask deeper questions about our work. Caught between the fiery heat and icy cold of creative engagement, we are asked to come to life in the tension between two opposites. We must make a hearth and home at the very place where the life we feel we are stuck with and the life we desire meet and overlap.

An eighth-century Zen master named Kukei summed up this meeting place of desire and acceptance with this fierce little poem. It is called, appropriately for this chapter, "Singing Images of Fire." This is a very fine translation by Jane Hirschfield.

> A *hand moves, and the fire's whirling takes different shapes.*
> *. . . all things change when we do.*
> *The first word, Ah, blossomed into all others.*
> *Each of them is true.*

Kukei takes a lifetime's journey in four lines. First of all, he says let's drop our complicated ideas about creativity. Just move your hand and fan the flames; with this one movement the whole universe moves with you. This may sound all too simple to our ears, but it is an assertion that the modern science of *complexity* would gladly second. Scientists now know that tiny movements have large cumulative effects on even vast systems. You want to know about creativity, Kukei says, move your hand, take a breath, make a sound. *All things change when we do.*

The first sound we make has tremendous possibility.

> *The first word, Ah, blossomed into all others.*
> *Each of them is true.*

Kukei is not saying that every sound we make, grumbling dyspeptically through the workday, can blossom into all others. First we must find our own *Ah!* Reciting this poem in a crowded auditorium, I always feel that Kukei's *Ah!* contains not only the *Ah Ah!* of discovery and revelation, of handing in the right report at the right time, but also the *Agh!* of driving to work through slow traffic on a gray Monday morning. Unless both sounds for both sides of experience are there, the meaning of the poem does not open. Kukei does not choose between these two realities, and from the encompassing breadth of his sound he includes the whole universe in his *Ah!* From this sound, which holds the quality of suffering with the simultaneous experience of breakthrough, everything can blossom and everything is true to Kukei's experience.

This is not just the experience of a Zen master after years of intensive meditation. One of the greatest pioneers of modern corporate America, Thomas Edison, seems to have had an exceptional understanding of the need to hold both the joyous and grief-filled sides of experience in one outlook. An astonishingly creative inventor and scientist with a real personal artistry, Edison seems to have been able to call on both the Apollonic and Dionysian sides of his psyche when faced with the frustrations and conundrums of invention.

Late in his life, Edison was working on a literal problem of illumination: how to construct a filament for his brand-new electric light bulb, one that would not burn out, as every material he tried seemed to, in the briefest of instants. He had had teams of experimenters working on the problem around the clock for months. Finally the foreman of the work teams came to him, cap in hand. "Mr. Edison, I am sorry to say we have done a thousand experiments and worked thousands of hours to find this filament and I am afraid to say, it has all been for nothing." Edison looked back at the man and said, "Nonsense, we know a thousand ways in which it doesn't work!"

Now, when we get to our deathbeds, and the proverbial grandchild asks us what our life was all about, Edison's phrase is probably the only thing we will be able to say with any certainty. "I know a thousand ways in which it doesn't work." This may be a conservative figure by that time of life, for by late maturity we are surely up into the fifteen hundreds on the measurable scale of mistakes. The point is that Edison's genius lay exactly in his ability to embrace failure as an essential part of the path of creation, something he was able to do not only by his approach but also in his very speech.

Some things cannot be spoken or discovered until we have been stuck, incapacitated, or blown off course for a while. Plain sailing is pleasant, but you are not going to explore many unknown realms that way. We articulate the truth of a situation by carrying the whole experience in the voice and allowing the process to blossom of its own accord. Out of the cross-grain of experience appears a voice that not only sums up the process we have gone through, but allows the soul to recognize in its timbre, the color, texture, and complicated entanglements of being alive.

> *The first word, Ah, blossomed into all others.*
> *Each of them is true.*

DECIPHERING THE FIRE

Creativity and the articulation of creative ideas have always been experienced as a form of combustion, as if the soul and the world it perceived have suddenly been set alight. Here is the Nobel Prize–winning poet Pablo Neruda, looking back to his first fiery but inarticulate attempt to write the poetry that would become his life's work. It is taken from a poem called "La Poesia," or "Poetry." To my mind, this short fragment of Neruda's poetry illustrates in a superb way the fiery path of creativity and the preservation of the soul's desires that occur when we find work that fulfills longings at a deeper level than material security.

> *I didn't know what to say, my mouth*
> *could not speak,*
> *my eyes could not see*
> *and something ignited in my soul,*
> *fever or unremembered wings*

and I went my own way,
deciphering that burning fire
and I wrote the first bare line,
bare, without substance, pure
foolishness,
pure wisdom
of one who knows nothing,
and suddenly I saw
the heavens
unfastened and open.

Trans. David Whyte

An electric description of the moment the soul enters into the gravity field of its own destiny. But the poet's world is not a special world, the specialness of Neruda's words lies in his ability to carry the experience in his speech. What he describes is a moment that is shared universally, on the mountainside or in the corporate office.

What is courageous in Neruda's poem is his willingness to begin firmly in the unknown. He intuits that a close relationship with silence and emptiness is essential. It is always tempting to think that our job description is our identity, but if we take the step that Neruda took, we must stop being so sure we know who we are.

I didn't know what to say, my mouth
could not speak,
my eyes could not see

There is an equivalent to this embrace of the unknown in the Eastern traditions, the fiery practice of *not knowing*. This is not a prescription for feigning ignorance but for cultivating a sharp and attentive mind not given to easy answers. In the contemplative traditions, not having easy answers to everything that comes along is termed *inner silence*. In the beginning, then, our ability to respond creatively, whether at our desks, on the production floor, or on the yet-unwritten page, depends on our ability to live with the unexplored territory of silence.

A real experience of silence is almost always fiery in nature. Anyone who has tried for inner quiet soon finds how desperately difficult it is to sustain it. Like a fretting accountant with his calculator, the mind is constantly going over the balance sheet of our opinions and prejudices, afraid perhaps we might forget them and lose sight of the bottom line that makes up our identity. Whatever our difficulties, learning to sustain this inner quiet is perhaps one of the more harrowing experiences the human soul goes through in its quest for deepening. It is difficult in a quiet monastic setting; at work it might seem impossible. We are a busy people in a busy corporate culture. But even the busiest person wants wisdom and sense in busyness.

As the current catchphrase goes, we want to work smarter rather than harder. Yet all of us are familiar with frantic busyness as a state that continually precludes us from opening to the quiet and contemplation it takes *to be* smart. The fast-moving mind rebels against slowing the pace because it intuits that it will not only have to reassess its identity but also take time to recover and recreate, and of course when we are in the buzzing-worker-bee mode, that would be a loss of momentum difficult to justify. We do not even have time to find out if our momentum is taking us over the nearest cliff.

If we are serious about the soul at work, and the creativity that sustains a soulful work life, all of us must confront the question of quiet and comtemplation in the workplace. But silence means many things to many people.

Having two children, my assistant finds the concentrated busyness of her mornings in my study-of-fice a kind of bliss. She is able to work in an uninterrupted flow not granted to a constantly needed parent. (Of course, parenthood offers far greater joys than anything working in my office can grant her. In giving ourselves fully to children we can, against all the odds, find silence even there too!)

Quiet and contemplation in the office does not necessarily have to be in the form of a special room for silence and meditation; it could equally be in the form of a company culture that encourages people to admit they do not always have an answer. There is, in effect, a real experience of silence that can emerge from that atmosphere. A spacious atmosphere of learning that encourages a quiet but extensive breadth of perspective.

So the state Neruda describes

> *I didn't know what to say, my mouth*
> *could not speak,*
> *my eyes could not see*

is not the description of a state of ignorance, but a numinous experience of inner quiet and an intuition of a new possibility coming to life in that silence. We notice that Neruda is able to sustain the silence even as his new life as a poet takes light:

> *and something ignited in my soul,*
> *fever or unremembered wings*

Like most of us caught in the first heady moments of creation, Neruda doesn't quite recognize what is occurring inside him, but the breadth of his silence allows the process to continue even through these turbulent early moments. He has room for new imagery even if it is an unfamiliar and feverish beating of wings. Without silence we become frightened by what is occurring. There is no room for it to grow inside us, and bereft of that spaciousness, we feel as if the process is about to take us over.

The next lines seem to hold the key to the kingdom of creativity. Neruda, tracing his path from that early breakthrough to his full maturation as an international presence in twentieth-century letters, lays out the one thing that made the difference in his life. It echoes Robert Frost's gentler poem in which two paths, one less traveled than the other, diverge in a yellow wood, but Neruda encapsulates it in a startling image:

> *and I went my own way,*
> *deciphering that burning fire*

Neruda's footsteps along the path less traveled are ones that few of us have the courage to follow, the courage to step into the self-respect and sharp attention that its alternatively nourishing and burning aspects require of us. To go our *own way, deciphering that burning fire.*

The magnificent phrase, *deciphering that burning fire,* shows Neruda's ability to treat life as a mystery to be lived rather than a problem to be solved, but it is easy to misinterpret the line following it, *and I went my own way,* as a suspiciously selfish tack, as if he meant to go his own way and the hell with the consequences. But we must remember the peculiar art that Neruda was giving himself to: poetry, that most intimate verbal art of human communication. For poetry to be poetry there must be a listener as well as a speaker. Neruda going his own way is not a rebel without a cause but a young man determined to make his way into the listener's ear. His solitary path, then, is faithful to something greater than the personal satisfaction of hearing his own voice. It is a soul-based relationship with the world revealed by his voice and his imagination.

The difficult part about writing poetry is that you must go your own way to write the poem. But having done that, the poem must belong to everyone—just as work must be useful and beneficial to others even as it satisfies the person engaged in it.

A bad poem belongs only to the writer (though it may make a fine journal entry), a well-made poem may include a circle of people who share the sensibility of the author, but a *great* poem pulls in everyone who reads it for generations to come. Some may be pulled into the poem, as many academics are, arguing and shouting, but the work itself is compelling, as if someone has suddenly said something out loud in a crowded room that must be listened to, answered, or argued about for years to come. My father, who shows very little everyday interest in poetry, can still recite, under the influence of a Sunday lunchtime in our local Yorkshire pub, lines from Wordsworth's "Daffodils" that remain in his mind from childhood lessons. What separates poetry from religious dogma is the ability of a poem to speak across time to everyone no matter their world view. An immortal poem, to use the old phrase, allows each person to enter the poem in their own way, even those not yet born.

> *and I wrote the first bare line,*
> *bare, without substance, pure*

> *foolishness,*
> *pure wisdom*
> *of one who knows nothing,*

Anyone not prepared to look a little foolish now and again would be better not starting this path. Any artist or manager worth their salt must be prepared to do bad art or be prepared to fail at a planned goal now and again. It is the same spirit that is called on when we brainstorm ideas, where no image or conception is off limits. You simply keep the stream of ideas flowing onto the butcher paper pinned around the room. The discipline lies in the ability to recognize the patterns emerging that are germane to the path you want to take. But this demands the courage to choose and to choose wrongly. The more we choose, the more we come to recognize and trust our own instincts, our "pure wisdom."

As a famous actor says about his craft: "The more I practice, the luckier I get." He means, no doubt, the spontaneous joy of having the character he was playing suddenly appear, as if from nowhere, fully formed.

> *and suddenly I saw*
> *the heavens*
> *unfastened and open.*

As the book of Proverbs says: "The desire accomplished is sweet to the soul." But these last lines are difficult lines. Neruda is experiencing the heaven of firsthand experience. He has nowhere to go and needs nothing else to feel complete. His experience of communion with the world is sufficient unto itself. "Behold the lilies of the field, they neither spin nor weave, yet verily I say unto you, Solomon in all his glory was never arrayed as one of these." Words sweet of a Sunday morning, yet heretical if spoken aloud to the beleaguered manager who has to work the rest of the week.

This aspect of the soul's firsthand, or heavenly, experience is a dangerous and difficult achievement in the workplace. We like the idea of heaven but feel safer when it remains the other side of existence. Something we'll get to when we are good and ready, after we are dead perhaps. Being dead helps; heaven, after all, means everything we ever wanted coming to meet us in one terrifying moment. The Greeks said that if the gods really wanted to punish someone, they granted that person everything they had wished for. This statement has a double edge to it; it is not speaking only to the timeless human ability to long for things that are detrimental to their souls, but to the equal difficulty humans have in receiving those divine gifts which offer the soul a moment of complete fulfillment. It speaks to the difficulty of experiencing joy. To enter heaven, to find joy in our work, simply entails giving up too much.

JOY IN THE WORK

In the Tibetan concept of heaven, detailed in the *Tibetan Book of the Dead*, the task of a person entering the transitional realms of death is to be able to recognize and identify with the Godhead when it approaches them. If they can do this, they are taken up by that divine entity into Nirvana and joyfully forgo the doubtful privilege of coming back for another human life. (And, we might say to ourselves, *another job.*)

Tibetan teaching, however, says that this numinous joining with heaven happens only rarely out of millions of lives and deaths. Most people find the representation of divinity so all-encompassing and frightening that they cannot let go of their previous images of what divinity should be. Heaven is suddenly perceived as the terrifying place where we are transparent to everything else, and where all our previous hopes and conceptions must be both seen and dropped. Heaven approaches us and is experienced as the most frightening thing the soul has ever seen. Better, we say, to go around for another cycle with all those things with which we are familiar. Better the devil you know.

So much for the *Tibetan Book of the Dead*, but this happens every day in office buildings across the country. The experience of joy is so incredibly rare in the workplace because it entails a constant giving up in order to even recognize the territory. We prefer to return to those states of seminumbness with which we are more familiar. The states of simplicity and timelessness are rarely known, because rarely looked for.

> *Not known, because not looked for*
> *But heard, half heard, in the*
> *stillness*
> *Between two waves of the sea.*
> *Quick now, here, now, always—*
> *A condition of complete simplicity*
> *(costing not less than everything)*

> T. S. *Eliot*, Four Quartets

The rare appearance of joy at work is so painfully exquisite that we may actually experience joy as a moment of terror. It opens to us all our possibilities and yet casts a shadow of comparison across all our other moments. Joy brings an intimation of death and mortality. This joy will pass as all others have before them. Laughter catches in our throat because we refuse to accept the corollary of joy, the soul-enriching poignancy of loss.

The experience of joy in the workplace means we are made more vulnerable to loss in a corporate culture where loss is the first bullet point on the important list of things *not* to be experienced. We feel there must be something wrong with the natural vulnerability that accompanies joy and refuse to harvest those moments which bring nothing to us but pure experience itself, where even failure is welcomed as the salt that gives flavor to the feast.

I wrote the following poem for an older friend who was going through something of a depression over his aging. The fleeting aspect of existence had passed across his face and left a shadow. It was written for him, but it was also written to the part of myself that will refuse the prospect of taking joy in my life because it also opens me to the prospect of losing everything that is most precious to me.

OPEN

It is a small step to remember
how life led to this
moment's hesitation.

How the door to the deeper world
opens, letting the body fall at last,
toward the few griefs it can call its own.

Oh yes, I know. Our wings catch fire
in that downward flight
and we come to earth afraid
we can never fly again.

But then we always knew
heaven would be a desperate place.
Everything you desired coming

in one fearful moment
to greet you.

Your full presence only in rest
and the love that asks nothing.
The rest where you lie down
and are no longer found at all.

The rest where we lie down and are no longer found at all. *Aware*, the Heian Japanese poets used to call it. The bubble world. An interpretation of existence and feeling that fills the body equally with sorrow as much as with joy. I feel it particularly in the joy my young son brings me. I do not feel equal to whatever hole his disappearance would make in my life, therefore I continually glimpse myself holding the subtle distances that preserve my safety. To fall toward him is to embrace the possible grief in that love, as falling toward our work we embrace the griefs and losses that have held us from the small everyday joys our soul loves to conjure from experience.

The soul's ability to experience heaven or joy in the corporate workplace, then, is commensurate with our ability to feel grief. What griefs? Grief in the daily struggle, grief in the neglect of family, grief in the continuing sacrifice of our precious personal time, all placed on the altar of the organization, and all of it never enough. We spend too much time rationalizing or justifying the way we work and too little time experiencing the griefs themselves. The result is that these griefs remain hidden and never open us to our joys. It is as if the two are simply two ends of the same whole. Remove the experience at one end of the scale by curtailing our capacity for grief, and the whole emotional body shrinks into a bland middle, curtailing equally our capacity for joy.

Jean Shinoda Bolen, in her book *Goddesses in Everywoman*, quotes writer Ardis Whitman's embrace of loss and solitude after the death of her husband. He had had a heart attack soon after giving her a brief hug and dashing out the door. He never returned to the house again. Seven years later she wrote:

Like the first thin sunlight after rain, there is a meager yet growing warmth that is as indigenous to unchosen solitude as sorrow itself is. It is warmed by memory . . . also by a growing sense of our own identity. When we live surrounded by people, some of the passion and insight natural to us leaks away through the sieve of small talk. At your most daring moments you believe that what is going on is the ultimate human work—the shaping of a soul. The power of life comes from within; go there; pray; meditate. Reach for those luminous places in your self.

It is the embrace of failure and grief, harrowing as these are, that forms the vessel for the joyous votive flame of creativity. Without this vessel in which to carry the fire, it is easy to breed a kind of whiz-kid arrogance and end up burning our hands.

In the eighties, many of those high-flying eternal

youths, untouched as yet by the embrace of personal loss, wearing bright ties and yellow suspenders, dismantled or saddled with debt any company they could get their hands on in order to gain another few feet of elevation. We find this disturbing motif in the ancient story of Icarus, who, using the wings made by his father, Daedalus, escaped the labyrinth of King Minos and flew higher and higher toward the sun, so high that he melted the wax that held together the feathers of his outstretched wings. He plunged into the sea, a victim of his own lust for altitude.

For many youths caught in the Wall Street crash of 1987, this heated plunge into cool water was a kind of tempering, and whether taking place in the psyche of an individual, a company, or society, signaled the beginning of newer, more sober, but thankfully saner times.

DROPPING INTO THE SEA

The 1980s already seem long, long ago. Yet we are still not sure what the nineties ask of us. We are spending less, traveling less, and finding our soul pleasures closer to home. This seems emblematic not only of economics, but of a turn toward soul life that many people are attempting. Even though most of us did not have the opportunity to fly high in the eighties, but only to witness its excess, we were all affected by the zeitgeist of that era, and we are only now beginning to surface from the stricken plunge of Black Tuesday that marked the end of that time. In the nineties we are being forced to come to terms with our arrogance after the eighties attempt to fly to the sun.

Dropping into the sea like Icarus, we are dropping into the more oceanic realms of existence, a place where any creative fire must burn in an interior form to survive underwater. We can think of this, for our organizational work, as the ability to stay in touch with our vitality and act accordingly, even when inundated by events. In the metaphor of water, this is Beowulf's time in the lake, when he grasps the luminous sword; in the metaphor of fire it is relinquishing our reliance on a constant fuel supply from the outside to keep our own fire going. We stop trying to fly toward the sun and discover another, more compressed, interior source of light.

As the Spanish poet Antonio Machado said,

> *Last night, as I was sleeping,*
> *I dreamt—marvelous error!—*
> *that there was a fiery sun here in my heart*
> *It was fiery because it gave warmth*
> *as if from a hearth*
> *and it was sun because it gave light*
> *and brought tears to my eyes.*

> *Trans. Robert Bly*

The sudden and intuitive capacity to feel deep emotion, what the romantic poets called *sensibility*, is the power of appreciation for *things as they are*. Creativity means first accepting creation as it is and then joining the embryonic flow of patterns and events we see emerging from its center. We learn to discern and decipher when to float in the subtle turn and flow, and when to strike boldly for shore, breaking through those flows and eddies as we go. We do this not only in the wide-open water of possibility and success, but also in the dark, still-water knowledge of our limitations and failures. Joining these together, we acknowledge the ever-present portion of existence that refuses to absolve us because we work for successful companies, from the cycles of florescence and decay. We find we do not have to be on top, in control, or in the driver's seat to feel we are participating, paid-up members of the world. We join the soul in its textured and maddening entanglement with everything that comes its way.

CONTAINED FIRE

Moving back to the image of flame, which began this chapter, we ground our creativity by making a hearth for our creative fire. With a hearth to warm the house in which we live, we have a place to rest at the center of things. There is long human relationship with the phenomenon of contained fire. It formed the basis of our ability to forge metal, to make exquisite Ming china, to propel a space shuttle beyond the clasp of our atmosphere, and, more soberly, to fire a bullet from a gun.

Contained fire is the vital force that we direct to accomplish firstly a task, but more importantly, a way of being. As the fire of our creativity burns its way into our interior life as much as it transforms the world at large, we experience what the medieval philosophers called the *alchemical wedding*, the meeting of the interior world of a single human being with the great soul of the world. This betwixt-and-between worlds is the very touchstone of creativity. It exists as much in a development plan as it does in a great canvas. At that border, the initial myopic concerns of the individual are burned away, firstly, in the endeavor itself and then in the annihilation that occurs where the two worlds meet. It is this self-forgetfulness for which human beings long; the dross of self-preoccupation is burnt away, leaving the pure gold of the ancient philosopher's stone, a numinous engagement where the soul is seated on the bridge between the world we imagine and envision and the world as we find it. Refusing to choose, we do not sacrifice our practical duties for the mere seductions of fire, but become tenders of the flame, using it to fuse and hold together elements that would fall apart at room temperature.

And all shall be well and
All manner of things shall be well

When the tongues of flame are in-
folded
Into the crowned knot of fire
And the fire and the rose are one.

T. S. *Eliot*, Four Quartets

The alchemists maintained that we can create only in our own image. That is, everything takes form according to the consciousness that shaped it. If our self-image is small and restricted, or cold and inert, then what we produce will most probably be stillborn, like its maker. It is essential then, to know what is vital and alive inside us and shape our lives in its image. With a leaden appreciation of ourselves, everything we make takes on that dull weight. To create the golden moment we must know where the gold lies in ourselves, but we must not have narrow, tidy images of what makes up our "gold." Without the fiery embrace of everything from which we demand immunity, including depression and failure, the personality continues to seek power *over* life rather than power *through* the experience of life. We throw the precious metal of our own experience away, exchanging it for the fool's gold of a superimposed image, an image of what our experience *should* be rather than what it actually is, the final element in the act of creation.

There is an ancient Chinese story of an old master potter who attempted to develop a new glaze for his porcelain vases. It became the central focus of his life. Every day he tended the flames of his kilns to a white heat, controlling the temperature to an exact degree. Every day he experimented with the chemistry of the glazes he applied, but still he could not achieve the beauty he desired and imagined was possible in the glaze. Finally, having tried everything, he decided his meaningful life was over and walked into the molten heat of a fully fired kiln. When his assistants opened up the kiln and took out the vases, they found the glaze on the vases the most exquisite they had ever encountered. The master himself had disappeared into his creations.

Work is the very fire where we are baked to perfection, and like the master of the fire itself, we add the essential ingredient and fulfillment when we walk into the flames ourselves and fuel the transformation of ordinary, everyday forms into the exquisite and the rare.

Fire in the Voice

Voice

Speaking Out at Work

A man I know finds himself in a meeting room at the very edge of speech; he is approaching his moment of reckoning and he is looking for support from his fellow executives around the table. Strangely, at this moment, no one will look at him. The CEO is pacing up and down on the slate-gray carpet. He has asked, in no uncertain terms, for their opinion of the plan he wants put through. "I want to know what you all think about this," he demands, *"on a scale of one to ten."*

The CEO is testy; he makes it plain he wants everyone to say *"ten,"* and damn whether they mean it or not. He is just plain tired, after all this time, of people resisting his ideas on the matter. He glares at them, he wants compliance. My friend thinks the plan is terrible and that there is too much riding on this solitary ego; everyone in the company will lose by it. He is sure also, from talk he has heard, that half the other executives in the room think so too. As they go around the shamefaced table, the voices of those present sound alternatively overconfident, or brittle and edgy. Most say *"ten,"* one courageous soul braves a *"nine and a half,"* and my friend is the last to go.

He reaches his hand toward the flame, opens his palm against the heat, and suddenly falters; against everything he believes, he hears a mouselike, faraway voice, his own, saying *"ten."*

Courageous speech has always held us in awe. From the first time we spoke back to our parents as angry, stuttering teens, or had to stand tongue-tied before a roomful of people, feeling naked as the day we were born. There is, after all, something bare and revealing about speech. Perhaps because we intuit the physical intimacy behind the sound of words and the way they are spoken, and that much against our wishes our words tell the listener a good deal more than we would have them know about us.

The voice emerges literally from the body as a representation of our inner world. It carries our experience from the past, our hopes and fears for the future, and the emotional resonance of the moment. If it carries none of these, it must be a masked voice, and having muted the voice, anyone listening knows intuitively we are not all there. Whether or not we try to tell the truth, the very *act* of speech is courageous because no matter what we say, we are revealed.

A courageous, soul-filled speech may simply mean accepting the consequences of being revealed. The courage to speak and stand by what we overhear ourselves saying is a learned and often frightening discipline. In the workplace, with all its fears and terrifying hierarchies of power, this courage is something every person feels compelled to learn. In my own tradition it is also central to the writing of poetry. In our first attempts at courageous speech, in the meeting room or on the empty page, we prepare to roar like a lion and deliver, instead, the timorous peep of a mouse. Our first thought is to withdraw from the mouse in horror. The Pulitzer Prize or the potential promotion cannot lie this way, we say to ourselves. But there is a place for the mouse. The mouse sound is a sobering sound because we come to realize that it is not something that suddenly rises up and embarrasses us at the wrong moment, but an essential part of our nature, an indicator of our hopes and fears. If mouse is all we have, then a first courageous step might be to say mouse is what we have to work with.

I cannot help but think of Robbie Burns' famous description of a timorous mouse he startled, painted forever in broad Scots dialect.

> *Wee, sleekit, cow'rin, tim'rous, bestie*
> *O what a panic's in thy breastie!*

Having startled the mouse inside ourselves, we might, for instance, see the mouse voice as an indication of where exactly our voice is hiding and in its minute, brittle sounds intuit a greater voice that lies behind it. We also learn something about the fears that lie behind our speaking out. The mouse is the part of us that learned how to hide between the walls of the house until nightfall, emerging when the master and mistress were asleep. A mouse sound heard in the light of day, then, is the first indication that our voice is coming out of hiding, though it may still be fearful of those we perceive to be rulers of our world.

Hearing the mouse emerge in a conversation at work, especially with someone who may have power over us, we are being reminded that Mother and Father are still very much present in our lives. In psychological language, we have stumbled into the complex that lies at the center of our relationship with our parents or anyone we come across with whom it is difficult to reveal ourselves in full. One of the definitions of our parents might be "those from whom my true life is kept," simply because our life tends to take us away from them, and the pain surrounding that is difficult for them to bear. But as we grow older and leave our parents, we still find ourselves keeping our lives sacrosanct from those who want control over us, from those who wish to make themselves a mother or father in our lives. But we may know how to keep that sacredness only through being a mouse. In poetic language, having heard the mouse, we then learn through those mouse sounds how to coax our mouse out of hiding, and begin, however hesitantly, to treat the world or the organization as a mythological equal, a peer instead of a parent, a co-partner on the path instead of an all-powerful provider or persecutor.

The practiced poet trying to speak to the world on equal terms becomes, for better or worse, very familiar with his own mouse sounds and finally comes to expect a fair amount of furtive scurrying and squeaking before the fuller qualities of the voice can open. But the first experience of the mouse can be heartbreaking. We want fire in our belly and our voice to meet the fire out in the world, but find everything that lies to hand damped by the feverish moisture of fear and self-loathing. The self-loathing is compounded because we feel we have finally been revealed for what we are. "I said *'ten,'* I must be a mouse." A man can literally hear the old question even as he speaks. "Are you a mouse or a man?" A woman hearing timidity in her voice might feel herself slipping back to the inherited role of pleasing others at all cost.

But there is another, more important aspect to mouse sounds. The frail, vulnerable sounds of which we are capable seem to be essential to a later ability to roar like a lion without scaring everyone to death. Without the compassionate understanding of the fear and trepidation that lie behind courageous speech, we are bound only to our arrogance. Lion sounds that have not grown from the mouse may exude naked power like the testy CEO but cannot convey any wisdom or understanding lying behind the voice. The roaring sound of someone like the CEO who has not come to terms with the fears of his or her inner mouse is almost always a form of preemptive attack, used against others as the best means of defense.

The initial steps on the path of courageous speech then, are the first tentative steps into the parts of us that cannot speak. Entering their shadowy, previously hidden abodes, we discover an interior soul energy that has not seen the light of day in a long time.

It has not seen the light of day because we find it hard to like what we hear when we first go in there. The singer beginning to work on her voice wants Maria Callas but doesn't find it. She finds her abdomen and chest will not open to carry the sound. The actor wants Richard Burton, but his round, golden tones have no undercurrent of grief and regret to match that of Burton. The person low on the office totem pole wants the voice of authority but has not yet found the place in his body where it resides. We want only one side of the equation, the same side of the equation that the overarching hierarchy of the corporation wants of *us*. Control, consistency, and predictability. Like the corporation, we want every voice but the cracked and slightly broken voice we must first call our own.

FINDING A VOICE

The voice, like the eyes and the face, is traditionally a window to the soul. If, as Gerald de Nerval said, the seat of the soul is not inside a person, or outside a person, but the very place where they overlap and meet with their world, then the voice is as good a candidate as any for getting the measure of our soul life. The voice carries the emotional body of the person speaking. Without verbal explanation, but simply through sound, it tells us *who* is speaking, and, in the meeting room, who has come to work. The voice is as important to our identity as anything we possess. We ask ourselves if we really have *a voice* in this organization, want reassurance that we can *give voice* to our opinions, and if we cannot, speak *soto voce* to those few in whom we choose to confide.

In the simple act of saying *ten* to those listening around the meeting table, we focus an interior current of air from the larynx out through a slight gap between our vocal cords. Like wind soughing through a high pass, the air resonates the cords and with the help of the tongue forms the words that order or break apart our existence. A woman's cords resonate at a higher frequency than the bass note of a man, but the throat, like a mountain pass, is only a focus for the moving current of air behind it. The sound itself is dependent on the fullness of the air mass that passes through that slender gap, and that fullness is made by the whole body.

Opera singers and performers quickly learn that sound is produced by the full length of the body. The lungs work in concert with the belly and the belly sits like a crossroads between the legs and the upper torso. The throat may be perfectly free, but sit down to sing and you will produce a different, more curtailed sound than standing. Open the chest, round the belly with the whole breath, drop your center of gravity, and plant your feet on the floor, and you will sound grounded and solid, a world away from your voice when you are strutting tensely on tiptoe. Not only that, but hearing the literal body language in these opposing voices, others will actually treat you differently, as if dealing with two entirely separate people.

The voice, after all, is entering the body of the listener and radically affecting his inner world. The word *ten*, for instance, is focused by the outer funnel of the ear, gathered on the membrane of the eardrum, and passed through a watchmaker's arrangement of three tiny bones to the salty fluid of the inner ear. This minuscule inner sea responds to sound the way the real sea responds to the moon, shifting with tidal currents hundreds of tiny hairs rooted in the auditory nerve cells. The emotional and imaginal world radiates out from those ear follicles through the whole length of the body on a tide of electrical impulses, warming the heart, sickening the stomach, or stimulating the adrenals in an instant to fight or flight.

Imagine if my friend had said, to the fury of the CEO, *zero*, on a scale of one to ten. There is a world of difference in the bodies of startled executives hearing *zero* pronounced into the room and those hearing a hesitant *ten*. The word *zero* would pass through the listeners like an emotional shock wave, galvanizing some to further acts of cowardice and others to the courage of their convictions; it brings to mind, like the Chinese pictograph for *crisis*, intimations of danger and opportunity, and the word *ten*, like a finger in the collapsing dike of truth, a feeling of futility. A kind of bodily and emotional shrinkage. But the *zero* would have to come from a person who was inhabiting his entire body, his belly as much as his throat. Otherwise, the *zero* comes across like a flagged semaphore of fear. It says to the assembled male executives, "I am not completely sure of myself, eat me, eat me now—one gulp!"

Inhabiting the full body, the long body, as many North American Native traditions say, with the voice, may be one of the great soul challenges of adult life. If the voice originates and ends its journey in the bodies of the speaker and listener, it is also true that many parts of our bodies are struck deaf or dumb from an early age. We walk through the door into the organization every morning looking like full-grown adults, but many parts of us are still playing emotional catch-up. The griefs and traumas of childhood follow us around, asking for attention. It is generally accepted in modern psychology that children suffering emotional trauma unconsciously refuse to grow any older until that trauma is resolved. They do not want to hear anything more on the matter; it is just too painful.

Or we might more accurately say that that *part* of a child which is traumatized or threatened refuses to grow older. The rest of the psyche may grow and mature, closing like a protective callus around the wound, but the wound itself remains isolated. This wound is more often than not located in a specific part of the body, one that can no longer speak. Certain voices inside us may grow and mature, others, when bad things happen to us, may act and sound, even in the company of fellow professionals, like a frightened seven-year-old. We look around at work and see outwardly self-possessed adults, but know from long experience that the layer of composure and control can be very thin. A professional environment seems especially conducive to the appearance of the wounded child. All the components of control and pleasing are present in good measure, ready to trigger the emotional allergic reactions that do everything but bring us out in a rash. We try to speak calmly in an emotionally charged situation and find ourselves struggling with the unconscious forces surging in the pit of our stomach.

As a child, a person may have disowned any feeling in the stomach area, for instance, having had their joyous breathy sounds constantly curtailed by the adult rulers of their world. A child shouts from its stomach, an adult jolts the child with a cutting phrase. The child experiences the worst of all scenarios in this disapproval, an irrational (or at times an all-too-accurate) feeling of love being withdrawn from them, as if forever. In fear of this, the child identifies the now-knotted stomach as the source of the problem, and withdraws from the quality the stomach can bring into the voice, refusing its gifts in order to forestall the possibility of returning to a place that seemed to cause the collapse of their world.

The result is that the voice lifts out of the belly and into the upper regions of the chest and the throat, where it is more in the grasp of the strategic mind and more amenable to being nice. Not being able to go through the painful door into the belly where an important part of the breath and the sound reside, the place in the body where we go to ground and earth our speech, we cannot get to its courageous rooted sounds when they are needed. To be able to say *zero* with conviction rather than fear needs the courage resident in the belly as much as it is resident in our convictions.

Saying the word *zero*, then, entails not just the pronunciation of a word but a reentry into neglected portions of the body that can uphold the challenge and stand by it. Our soul, at this point, if we are dealing with the stomach, literally depends on the courage resident in our guts. A courageous word itself is an act, and a word spoken with the whole body the literal wish to *embody* that act.

There is of course, a place for saving one's ammunition, for choosing one's battles, working under cover. There is a price to be paid for that strategy, but sometimes it may be justifiable. The point here is that to my friend, this *was* a battle worth fighting. This was the time to find out if he had a voice. He had seen that it was time to stake his claim and speak decisively despite the obvious consequences. His courage failed him at that moment, because he realized that the part of him that would say *zero* wanted a different life and destiny from the one he had now and *he was not yet ready to change*. The fire of enthusiasm for this new life, he suddenly realized, would burn the house of his present identity to the ground. He saw in an instant that he was not prepared yet to leave the comfort to which he had become accustomed. He was just as afraid of that voice saying *zero* as the CEO was. Recounting the story later, he said, in knowing self-reflection, "You bet your life I said *ten*."

The people who hear themselves say *zero* do not have the same life ahead of them as those who gave the hesitant *ten*. Saying *zero* literally means they have guts, and their voice is resident in their guts. They have a vessel to hold their fire. They have a stomach for the consequences, a place to which their voice can belong no matter the outward change in circumstances. Ambition is not rejected, but placed in the greater perspective of the soul, which again and again seems to choose a fuller experience of the here and now over a preordained trajectory through the corporate heavens.

The executive who is ambitious at all costs finds himself ritually killed by the sharpness of his own voice; the right word, said almost against his will, at the right time. Out of that annihilation arises another person, wilder, less predictable to others but more trustworthy to himself, stepping out on and deciphering a path he could at last call his own. But the courage in saying *zero* comes from the fact that we have only a hazy intuition of that person now coming to life who will pick up the pieces and carry on. It demands a simultaneous familiarity with two opposing sides of ourselves when we are more used to choosing one and ignoring the other.

My friend had already figured out in his *mind* that the CEO's plan was not a good one. But the fire in our belly literally goes out until we find the courage or the circumstance to walk back into those parts of our bodies we have disowned, and claim their earthy, grounded qualities for our own again. Sometimes we have so disowned our bodies in the cerebral machinations of the organizational world that a phrase like *Walk back into the body* may be a noncompute. I *am* in my body, we say, where else is there to be? But the question must then be Which body? The body we use like a machine to get everything done, or the body Blake described as ". . . the chief outlet of the soul in our age?" The body as an entangled way of perception and experience, or a door set against the world? Blake himself worked all his life, through art and poetry, to open up that door.

If the doors of perception were cleansed everything would appear to man as it is, infinite.

For man has closed himself up, til he sees all things thro' narrow chinks of his cavern.

William Blake, "The Marriage of Heaven and Hell"

William Blake, like my friend in the meeting room two hundred years later, had to walk back into his

own body, into his own unconscious physical memories, to cleanse the muddy doors of perception and
articulation. Arriving there, Blake found them shut
against him. He describes this in a brilliant but sobering poem called "The Garden of Love."

> *I went to the Garden of Love*
> *And saw what I never had seen:*
> *A chapel was built in the midst,*
> *where I used to play on the green.*
>
> *And the gates of this chapel were shut,*
> *And 'Thou shalt not' writ over the door;*
> *So I turned to this Garden of Love,*
> *That so many sweet flowers bore.*
>
> *And I saw it was filled with graves,*
> *And tomb-stones where flowers should be,*
> *And priests in black gowns were walking their rounds*
> *and binding with briars my joys and desires.*

We turn to our inner garden and find it full of dead
bodies, closed, and with a sign over the door of a
chapel. THOU SHALT NOT!

> *And priests in black gowns were walking their rounds*
> *and binding with briars my joys and desires.*

Unable to enter the garden, the wounded child remains in limbo, its desires bound by briars, unable to

experience the joys of its birthright or to grow into maturity with the rest of the adult psyche. It finds that a mode of being it was forced to employ during a stressful period when young, simply in order to survive, has become part of the imprisoning personality of the grown adult.

Children or not, we all have experience of this trauma to the body and the difficulty in opening those parts of ourselves which clanged shut so firmly in order to survive. It is a common but disturbing experience to hear our voice revert to old childhood timbres when we are put into fearful or vulnerable situations. Caught in the tension of a high-stress presentation, we might find ourselves playing out the same essential soul-struggles we had as children with our parents or teachers, especially with those figures of authority who now dominate our work lives. Blake's "priests in black gowns" are with us internally; we carry them with us wherever we go. If we do not find them literally in another person, we will project them onto those who look as though they might do at a pinch.

Every manager has had to deal with people who are absolutely allergic to any kind of direction, seeing in a simple request the hand of an internal bully with whom they have yet to come to terms. We carry these internal taskmasters with us because the soul is desperate to speak its desires in their presence and thus be freed from their rule. Until then, the part bound with briars can never escape, experience joy, or grow to maturity.

The psychological view of this situation would be to say that we are projecting our fears onto parental figures, particularly those at work whom we feel have power over us, and must overcome this tendency. But the soul's view might be to see these traumas as constantly repeated opportunities for courageous articulation, opportunities that the soul takes endless pains to engineer and place in our way until we step back through the doors of perception, back into the life promised to us before we sealed ourselves outside. We may think we are in the meeting room to preserve our job and our career, while at bottom the soul is making another bid for firsthand experience through courageous speech. It has no interest in being right; it simply intuits another life in the word *zero*. Folded in on itself by our strategies for survival, it is trying to open as much of its hidden interior surface area as possible.

As Rilke said, "Where I am folded in upon myself, there I am a lie."

I remember walking with a companion on a lonely road outside the small town of Otavalo in northern Ecuador. Turning a corner, we stumbled without warning into a wayside celebration of Otovalan Indians drunk on corn beer. Catching sight of us, they turned very nasty very quickly, suddenly surrounding and threatening us with fists, rocks, and machetes. I recall using every ounce of my silent will to hold them at bay while we walked through them on that dusty road, both of us, as far as I could see, marching toward a very violent end. We walked for what seemed an eternity like this, saying nothing as they worked themselves into an ecstasy of pent-up hatred at our presence. At the moment when the shouts and threats were reaching fever pitch, a ramshackle bus appeared out of nowhere, careening toward us over an open field. It stopped within running distance, and with a sudden shout we sprinted toward its door, pounding up its steps as a fusillade of rocks and missiles thudded against the metal sides of the bus.

Saved by this rusted angel of deliverance, I spent the next two days confined to my bed with stomach pains. The pains were incredibly sharp and the trauma of that strained confrontation with the angel of death so strong that I could feel my body revolt against the ruthlessness of a world that would kill me as soon as look at me. It was focused on my stomach perhaps because the truth was so hard to digest. I had done or said nothing that could have warranted attack; as an individual, my intentions were entirely good, but there was nothing my individual presence could do to stem the inheritance of five hundred years of exploited bitterness.

I remember noting, soon after my convalescence, that my voice had changed. It was no longer up in my throat, ready to be given away and please others so readily. It settled into my stomach along with my breath, bequeathing me a weight and acceptance in my voice that I had not previousy known. But there was also a troubled quality underneath that acceptance that did not make it passive. My voice could suddenly allow the presence of darker hidden energies I had previously left unexplored.

It was as if my stomach had held my breath and voice at a distance until that time, not wishing to be reminded that the process of living itself is a form of violation. I was, in Rilke's words, folded in on myself in self-protection against a terrible truth. We are born half strangled and choking for air, grow up invaded by sickness, are battered by mortgages, unwanted bills, and difficult circumstances as adults, and in old age must prepare for the ultimate violation and indignity of the hospital deathbed. In effect, the traumatic circumstances on that South American road opened, against my will, a part of my body long closed, and through the pain of that opening I was enabled to walk back in and inhabit a part of myself I had long neglected. It involved not only taking on new powers, but the giving up of my youthful illusions of immunity.

SAYING NO AS A PATH TO SOUL

Letting go of our immunity as the be-all and end-all of our lives, we claim the troubled but integral voice of the soul, ready to say the strangest, most eccentric things at the opportune moment and change our lives in an instant. But there is a method to its madness. The same voice that will say *no* to the CEO will also say *no* to the new car and the larger house that make us scared to death of losing our income and thus render us powerless to speak out. Not that the soul is puritanical about our expenditures, but if the voice is embodying the soul's desires it will say *no* again and again to the false seductions that lead us off on the path of fear and material aggrandizement.

If we have little idea of what we really want from our lives, or what a soulful approach to our work might mean, then often the only entrance we have into soul comes from the ability to say a firm *no* to those things we intuit lead to a loss of vitality. This way is traditionally known as the *via negativa*, or negative road, not to be confused with those contemporary deadly sins in the organization of negativity or pessimism. The *via negativa* is the discipline of saying *no* when we have as yet no clarity about those things to which we can say *yes*. We take the *via negativa* when there is not yet any sign of the *via positiva*. But in the continuous utterance of the *no* is a profound faith that the *yes* will appear. Not only is it bound to turn up by the law of averages, but it will also appear *because* we have said *no* to so much. In a way, if we treat our destiny as a potential marriage, it chooses us as much as we choose it, and like a seeker for our hand, deems us to be serious about it through our continued refusal of the wrong suitors. We create in effect a kind of energetic vacuum into which something we recognize can appear. Eventually appearing like an old and loving memory, it becomes all the more recognizable and real for its long absence.

This experience of a kind of deep memory may be more real to us than a thousand new experiences one after another. As T. S. Eliot wrote in a brilliant and painstaking way:

> I said to my soul, be still, and wait without hope,
> For hope would be hope for the wrong thing: wait without
> > love
> for love would be love of the wrong thing; there is yet
> > faith
> But the faith and the love and the hope are all in the
> > waiting.

One way to come to *yes* is to say *no* to everything that does not nourish and entice our secret inner life out into the world. As Rilke said, again:

> I want to be with those who know secret things
> or else alone.

We say no in order to bud and blossom in our own time, when saying yes might force us like a hothouse flower into a premature and evanescent bloom. We guard the richness of our interior hopes and imaginings even when there as yet seems to be nothing in the outer world that confirms them. When finally we do blossom, we may bear fruit in the most surprising and astonishing way.

NO BECOMES YES

Some years ago, during a weekend course I helped to lead in the south of England, I experienced a moving example of how the *via negativa* can blossom. The course was unusual for me, to say the least, in that I was the only man working amongst thirty-three Medical Missionary Sisters. The weekend was part of a six-week rest and recuperation for missionary nuns who had returned exhausted from their work in the hinterlands of Peru, Indonesia, India, and whatever other country needed the benefit of their good work and clinics.

Their work was difficult and exhausting, delivering babies, inoculating children, caring for the old and sick. You could not fault their endeavors, yet, as they say in the Christian tradition, they were all Martha and no Mary. They had absolutely no way of replenishing themselves. The Medical Missionary Sisters had little or no inner contemplative or prayerful discipline in their daily work. Every nun who went out worked herself into the ground for two years and then came back completely depleted. Working with the sisters, you could not help but be moved by their work and in despair at the mere shadows they had made of themselves to do it.

Down in the kitchen of the convent all the while, like Cinderella among the ashes, hidden away from our seminar room, was the young woman who served our meals every day. I say young, for although she seemed to be about twenty-seven years old, it transpired in our conversations that she was in her early forties. I was amazed, not only by her youthfulness, but by the glowing spirit of calmness and serenity she had about her work. It became the high point of each day, almost like a privilege to go down there and spend a few minutes with her as she served out the food. She seemed like a bright, shining light in the dim underground dining hall, and she never had a bad word for anything or anyone. It turned out that she had been a member of the Poor Clare order for over twenty years. The Poor Clares are a silent, prayerful order with an almost Zen-like approach to spirituality, spending much of their time in silent contemplation. She had entered the order at eighteen and spent more than two decades in contemplation; even the work of the convent was done by the sisters all working in mutual silence. Finally after twenty-three years, alone in her cell, she had heard an inner voice telling her to go out in the world and work on the behalf of others.

Following that voice without hesitation, she had joined the order that was hosting our weekend and come to the convent as part of her initial training.

The whole experience was something of a culture shock for her, but she had not a bad thing to say about her new order, though its whole approach was foreign to her training. There was not a trace of spiritual materialism in her body. I would hear her apologize to the others for appearing to ignore them when she worked in silence. "It's hard for them," she would say, "so I must keep explaining that silence means something else to me." Not a shred of judgment on her part as to their lack in the art of contemplation.

Witnessing her profound spiritual presence, I couldn't help but think that here was a woman who would never burn out no matter how much she applied herself to the outer world. She had an inexhaustible inner light that would endure through the direst of circumstances. She had come to that light through the ability to say *no* to everything except the thing most precious to her, an inner focus based on her personal spirituality and the religious life to which she had given herself. Out of those years of saying *no*, blossomed a magnificent *yes*; magnificent because she would be nourishing much more than the physical health of those she would care for—a *yes* that could be followed fully because after all those years gathering her psyche into one single body of faith, every part of her would be uttering it. *Yes!*

Though the other sisters were saving lives every day, the overwhelming feeling was that they were doing this work because there was something wrong with the world that needed to be put right, whereas this youthful hidden saint was doing it because every-thing was right about the world and she wanted others to experience it that way too. Her faith in her natural unfoldment and her own *no* took her to the farthest end of aloneness and then led her back in a moving return to human community. She, of course, would have made none of the fuss that I have made about her journey, for her it was one step at a time, one word at a time, one silence at a time for twenty-three years.

Though the average life in corporate America has little of the natural sanctity found in the vows of reli-gious life, the same internal imperatives work through each of us no matter our surroundings. Our soul and our personal destiny are equally at stake whether we are articulating our life in the corporation or the cloister. If we make our life vows consciously, we must speak them again and again in order not to forget. If they are as yet unconscious, the soul will work to uncover them by pushing us toward situations which demand us to explain ourselves. We can look at the pressures of corporate life in a pathological sense, stressful without sense or sensibility, or we can see it as the tempering element that unites the articu-lation of personal destiny with the urgent and prag-matic concerns of the everyday. We cultivate an inner life knowing that what is most important to us must be spoken and made real in the outer world, and in doing that we also gain a hard-won respect for the inner life and visions of others and the courage it takes to speak them in our presence.

By saying *no*, when we can, to many of the activities and things that come our way, we are continually thrown back on ourselves. By learning who is at the center of all this activity, we find inside ourselves someone who can say *yes* and at the same time be truly wholehearted. In the corporate world there is so much pressure to say *yes*, even if we are only halfway there. Disapproval from the wrong quarter can be deadly for prospects and advancement. Our intuitive reaction may be *no*, but without a full-bodied reply to back it up, we dislike simply sounding negative. Yes or no, the voice throws us back on what we want for our life. It forces us to ask ourselves Who is speaking? Who came to work today? Who is working for what? What do I really care about?

Our voice, then, is a powerful arbiter of our inner life, our power relationships with others, and a touchstone of faith in the life we wish to lead. In the office we can experience the disciplines of speech, and the inner silence from which good speech appears, as a measure of soul in our lives. Sometimes the voice is cowardly, sometimes courageous, and more often somewhere between the two, but whatever its outward appearance, tempered by the pressures of organizational life it represents the urgencies, desires, or emotional strangulation of a soul longing to be heard in the world.

Fionn and the Salmon of Knowledge

Innocence and Experience in Corporate America

If a fool would persist in his folly, he would

become wise. —WILLIAM BLAKE

W henever we try to speak up in the organization we reveal the precarious balance of innocence and experience in our voice. Too much innocence and we are sensed as "dangerous idealists," too much experience and we may sabotage everything we touch with a practiced cynicism. The corporate world is a marvelous touchstone for the troubling subjects of innocence and experience. Organizations trigger many of the struggles we experienced in youth with regard to our parents. In corporate life, innocence has to do with making our own way in the world whatever the odds stacked against us, while experience has to do with learning and understanding the power relationships that dominate our organizations. The corporation is at once the larger body that allows the individual to achieve things that are beyond his or her powers alone *and* the parent who tells the child exactly how things are going to be. The corporation both dispenses power to the individual and renders that same individual powerless. What kind of creative life can hold a bridge between the two without caving in to the engulfing parental system or leaving in anger to find supposedly greener pastures?

This is not a question confined to modern work life. Men and women have been riding out the contrary seas between the passions of innocence and the seductions of security for millennia. There are many old stories and much poetry that deals with this dilemma. At the heart of the dilemma is the way we set up our younger passionate selves against our older knowledgeable selves and our hard-won wisdom against the innocence that revealed that wisdom to us in the first place.

One of the finest stories grappling with the balance between the innocence and experience comes from the Irish tradition. It was told from generation to generation for almost two thousand years in the great halls of the Gaelic nobility, but I have also heard it told breezily, almost conversationally, as if it all happened yesterday, in a small, run-down pub in the west of Ireland—the story of Fionn's strangely idyllic boyhood and his coming to maturity through his eating of the Salmon of Knowledge.

THE ALIENATION OF INNOCENCE: THE SOUL AT RISK

Fionn's father, Uail, had been killed by his hereditary enemies, the sons of Morna. Now they wanted to put an end to Uail's line and began the hunt for Fionn himself, Uail's only son. That is how Fionn came to be raised by his mother's two sisters, far from human dwelling, in the wooded wilds of the west of Ireland.

If we are discouraged by the alienation of the contemporary workplace, we might take comfort from a long-held belief that the soul's journey begins when it realizes the true nature of its aloneness, that it has in effect been orphaned and must discover its true parentage. Amidst the pressures and politicking of the organization we ask the same questions: How did I get here? Do I really belong? What inner vision and purpose (or lack of it) brought me into his company? Realizing we are orphaned, we also come to terms with our need for the parental embrace of the organization.

An Irish friend of mind who, in the nature of his race, combines the priesthood, a great love of talk, and a formidable doctorate in German philosophy, turned to me once over a pint of Guinness, looked me right in the eye and said, "Do you know, that if we human beings really knew how alone we were, we would know a terror we had never even begun to experience before?" Coming from a man of the cloth, I was struck by his courage and the reluctance to reassure easily at the expense of deeper truths. Lowering my own glass slowly from my mouth, I stared at him, inspired by the moment, offered him more of the same. "My God, yes, and if we knew how joined at the hip we were, we would be terrified too." In the sobering silence that followed, the laughter and background talk of the pub took on an existential import as if hollow and full at the same time.

Our struggles with innocence and experience in an organization are much the same. We want to attain a balance point between two ends of the extremes, innocence and experience, aloneness and to-getherness, and find, if we do manage to attain it, a bland bureaucratic middle that knows nothing of either. The full terror of our aloneness is the force that makes us praise the meeting with others. The terror of intimacy and belonging gives us the depth and appreciation for aloneness. The soul's journey, even in the most faceless corridors of a large corpora-tion, is the winding, downward path into a depth of experience where our aloneness and intimacy with others are held to be indivisible.

But our journey to maturity begins when we first separate from our parents and come to our aloneness. We suddenly realize that mother and father are no longer there to pick up the pieces, that working for IBM does not guarantee a job for life, that the Ameri-can "dream," must be redefined, redrawn, and real-ized by each generation. We are, in effect, both nurtured into certain dreams and then orphaned from them each generation.

That is how Fionn came to be raised by his mother's two sisters, far from human dwelling, in the wooded wilds of the west of Ireland.

The early Irish took these harsh orphaning qualities of the world into account and built into their society an elaborate system of fosterage. At a certain age a child was sent away to be raised by another family. Besides forestalling feuds between clans who were bound by raising each other's children, it took the burden of the child's development off the shoulders of the nuclear family. It was understood that simply from an emotional point of view it is very difficult for a father or mother alone to initiate their own sons and daughters into the adult world. Being so close, and sharing the same psychological weaknesses, at the last moment they would conspire unconsciously to ignore what must be truly faced.

Our first day at work may mark the beginning of a particularly harsh fostering. For many of us there may be nothing there except the start of a long and lonely struggle. But the story of Fionn is concerned with the circumstances that lead to the soul's fulfillment in the world. If you want to prepare children to be fostered early in life, and to stand up for themselves and what they want, the story says, learn not only the nurturing power of the feminine but its fierceness too. As a solid first step Fionn is passed into the hands of powerful feminine energies, represented by the two druid sisters, to learn the essential lessons that will prepare him for his destiny.

This fostering was seen as the source of Fionn's inner strength. James Stephens's version of the story begins by saying, "He was raised by women, and there is no wonder in that, as it is the pup's mother teaches it to fight." The story begins, therefore, by placing the human spirit in the place of being hunted by our father's enemies, split from the mother and father but nurtured by the mother's sisters in the wild. That is a way of saying that we have inherited our struggles from our father and our mother but that in some essential way they will be powerless to help us deal with them. To the Irish, some other, wilder feminine knowledge, independent of motherhood, was needed to initiate us into the deeper urgencies of life.

Many personal struggles run from generation to generation within a family, like a dark underground river along which everyone floats, refusing to go beneath the water. As children, at one time or another in our growing lives, this underground spring inadvertently breaks to the surface of the family. One day we look into the face of our formerly all-powerful mother or father and see in their eyes, for the first time, the terrifying specter of defeat. Even if we cover up the moment in an instant, the knowledge of our aloneness is like an arrow through the heart. We see, in effect, what seems to be our hereditary enemy, the fear of not belonging, and like Fionn hiding from the sons of Morna, we know our very lives are at stake. At the moment we sense our vulnerability to powers in the world greater than our parents or our company, we are fostered out into the world against our wills, and we are dependent on what is there to receive us.

THE SOUL OUTSIDE OF TIME

Fionn grows from infant to boy, being taught not only by his mother's sisters in the arts of story, poetry, and hunting, but by the shifting movement of the seasons, and the minute lessons of the natural world in which he lives. Above all, he learns how to see, to listen, and to feel. The description is an old one of idyllic timelessness. It may be that many of the human myths, legends, and creation stories of a past golden age are the placing of this childhood vision into a mythical context, a childhood vision that may seem far from our daily work experience, but one which underlies much of our agony at the *lack* of time in the accelerated world of the corporation.

In the Zen tradition they say, "We study the self to forget the self." It may be that the child has a vision of the world that has not yet crystallized into *self* and *not self.* This is not to say that childhood is by definition idyllic; many of us carry remembered horrors of the loneliness and powerlessness of that time. But whatever timelessness we did experience somehow lives on inside, and refuses to die, whether brought to the surface of our present busy work lives or not. As a way of reminding ourselves, we tell stories that carry the timelessness encoded in their details. Story-telling evolves as an art partly because we become self-conscious or wisely tired of our own personal story as the final arbiter of reality. Tired of placing ourselves at the center of the world, we tell a story to say the same thing in a more embracing context. We say, "The boyhood of Fionn" or "The Garden of Eden" or "Once in Royal David's City."

Fionn is the portion of each of us that understands physically what it means to live in eternity, where *eternity* is not an endless amount of time but an experience outside of time, free from the stress of never being enough or having enough, a numinous experience of the present where we forget ourselves in the consummation of the moment. Perhaps more importantly, Fionn is the part of us that refuses to forget that experience. His story takes us through a series of initiations to a seminal moment of self-knowledge.

Fionn grows to maturity in the shadow of threat, and in his growing strength as a youth the storm clouds of jealousy whipped up by the sons of Morna began to gather about him, until, deciding his place of hiding could no longer protect him, and called by his future, he sets off into the world.

INNOCENCE IN THE WORLD OF EXPERIENCE

Taking the path out of his hidden and idyllic valley, Fionn, the soul of youth, came upon a traveling band of equally youthful poets homeward bound from their arduous training. Joyful at the prospect of a such entertaining companions and caught by their songs and poems, Fionn joins the merry band and matches them with the skill of his verse. Trading stories and news, they travel the rest of the day until they come to a low-lying swamp, where they decide to stop and rest. In the heat of the summer, all the band except Fionn are soon half asleep, dead to the world, when out of the marsh thicket appears Call Mac Cona, a bandit of terrible strength, who without mercy, and with his sword, cuts down the young poets in their sleep and rounds on Fionn for the kill.

The first entrance of the adult male world into Fionn's life is in the guise of the slayer of youthful innocence. Many of us can look back on our own youth to a company of friends who showed great promise and gifts and were one way or another slain by the adult world, either literally in the Vietnam War, or more subtly by the debilitating pressures of law school or a high-pressure corporation. The male corporate world is a particularly fierce teacher when it comes to this initiation. Many of the youths it has slain are still standing in upright positions, carrying out orders to the letter, enduring their work as a form of living death.

THE SOUL DECLARES ITSELF

Fionn made no attempt to run but looked straight into the eye of the bloodthirsty man who was surely about to finish him. Unnerved, Call Mac Cona hesitated for a moment and shouted, "Who are you?"

"I am Fionn . . . the son of Uail, son of Baiscne," shouted the youth. The red, swollen mouth of his attacker fell open. His hard eyes grew moist and wild. "In God's name, my captain's son," cried Call.

In the shape of this itinerant murderer, Fionn had met one his dead father's lieutenants, now clanless and fugitive, preying violently on the edge of a society that offered no home. "He was at war," says Stephens," with a world which had dared to kill his chief."

This description of Call reminds me of a vivid conversation I had with a very bitter man in the cafeteria of a large telecommunications company. His mentor and sponsor had been sacked that very day, and he viewed the surviving executives who had engineered his mentor's demise as his enemies. I could feel the palpable hatred in this man. His career at a dead end, he was ready to spring out of the thicket and swing his sword at whatever he found. His chief weapon of defense was a sharp-edged and destructive cynicism. I imagine that any young, newly hired person who had to work with him would suffer the same fate as the young poets in the story of Fionn. In effect, not having any connection with his own inner sponsor, his soul, this man felt completely betrayed when his outer sponsor disappeared and would kill everyone in his path by way of revenge.

Call, at least, recognizes a true outer representation of his soul in the shape of Fionn. "Will I not be your man," says Call, "and teach you all the cunning that I know?"

"You will," says Fionn firmly, and accepts his hand. At a crucial moment Fionn must declare his lineage, or he will be killed. He must know from whom he is descended, where his strength comes from, and what kind of blood flows in his veins. Otherwise that part of the world which has been orphaned without any training or preparation will kill him out of its own grief and alienation.

In our inner cities we see gangs of fatherless youths attempting to initiate one another with no older men in sight. When they finally look the adult world in the eye, they cannot answer the life-or-death question in the same way. "I am Fionn . . . the son of Uail, son of Baiscne." Having no familial destiny to bind them, they float into the streets, victims of random drive-by shootings or anonymous drug deaths. At present, an astounding fifteen percent of our young male population is in the corrective system, the instinctual wish for the older male replaced unconsciously in the guise of the prison guard.

But equivalent drive-by shootings occur every day in the corporate office. One deadly manipulative conversation or maneuver can finish a life's ideals in a moment. Young spirits can shrivel and die on contact when ambushed by the orphaned and disowned shadows of many corporate cultures. The story says that if you are like these young and idealist poets and have only a mental concept of idealism or ethics without the sustaining power of a deeper blood-remembering, then you are not long for this world, you are destined to fail the test when it comes, destined, like the young poets or the orphaned telecommunications executive, for disappointment and the life of cynicism and victimhood.

The connection to personal passion and destiny must be a physical one, felt in the gut. This kind of living relationship with personal passion can be extremely difficult in the antiseptic environment of a modern office. Its clean lines do not easily reflect the hidden pulses of human longing and remembrance.

Fionn's shout of belonging is not just the ability to know or remember literally who his forebears were, but a signal that he recalls his bodily intuitions of destiny, a quality rarely perceived clearly but nonetheless intuited in an almost physical way, a beckoning uncertainty, a gravity field of awakened desires. Fionn has this on call, literally at his fingertips.

William Blake, working alone in his engraving shop, refused to be bowed even by long years of poverty, and kept his fingers on the living pulse of this desire. Speaking of his own work and destiny, Blake said:

> *My fingers emit sparks of fire*
> *with expectations of my future labours*

Fionn would be about fifteen years old at this moment, brim full with expectation for his future labors.

His apprenticeship with the female side of his lineage over, he joins Call in his fastness in the moist woods and learns the ways of an older man. "And because it is hard," says Stephens, "for a man to keep a trick from a boy." Call taught him everything he knew. He even showed him, hidden in the wood, a spear so given to the spitefulness of killing that it had to be tied to a tree and bound tightly with cloth. It was exquisitely made and held together by thirty rivets of Arabian gold. He told Fionn that this weapon was not to be used unless his very life was at stake.

Often a mentor will take on a younger person but refuse to show the young man or woman this spear. They may never have been shown it themselves. Corporate ethics often seem to swing between two extremes, on the one hand outright ruthless avarice, and on the other a reliance on bland and bloodless middle-class ethics. The first one usually issues from the boardroom, the second from the Human Resources Department. One says the spear is to be used all the time or someone at some time will use it on you, while you are not looking; the other denies its existence altogether and says we have only to work together and everything will be all right.

The story of Fionn says that the spear is hidden in the thickets of existence, in the shadow of our ethics and best hopes for humanity. Convince yourself that it is not there and can be ignored and you will either be its victim or destroy everyone in range when you lose control and unbind the restraining cloth through anger. Many aspirations for a "kinder, gentler" business world founder at the first glimpse of this spiteful weapon at the center of human experience. Build the kind of world you want, says Call, but remember the spear and don't unbind it until your mind is clear and the time is right for its peculiarly ruthless presence. Even the kindest managers face the telling moment when they must fire an inefficient but otherwise likable employee. They *know* that the man or woman will suffer tremendous emotional and financial pain, but the situation can no longer be sustained. If they have been wisely told where the spear lies and when to use it, they untie the cloth for the moment it is needed and then are able to bind it up again just as quickly.

THE DANGERS OF YOUTH
WITH YOUTH

Fionn stayed with Call in the swamp, until the older man, mellowed by the renewal of his former family, had taught him all he could. With promises of future service, Fionn left Call's company and journeyed along the byways of Ireland until he came upon a group of boys playing at the edge of a broad river. Elated by their bold play and happy to find boys his own age, he struck up with them.

At first they were glad to have the young stranger with them. His abilities to run, jump, sing, and wrestle were far above them all. He became a hero to them. It is here, in fact, that he earns the name by which we know him—Fionn, which means "The Fair One." Stephens describes the essence of this name-giving in a marvelous way. "His name came by boys, and will, in the end, perhaps, be preserved by them." But soon, as young boys will, they grew jealous of Fionn's powers in everything he did and began to plot against him.

Having served his initiation with an older man, Fionn is wise to the dangers lurking in a crowd of young boys left to themselves. One of the prices we pay in the segregation of education by age is the self-referential reality that each class year and generation makes for itself. There is nothing more conservative and repressive in this world than the peer pressure of teenagers determined to enforce the unwritten codes of their world. The peer pressure among teenagers in American schools is often toward mediocrity. Anyone who excels academically may often earn themselves the label of nerd, which denies them the approval of the group. At the first scent of a plot against him, Fionn leaves them to go his own way.

THE SOUL CHOOSES ITS TIME

Having left the mythological equivalent of the street gang or the high school clique, Fionn first makes his way to the land of King Finntraigh, where he impresses the court with his hunting. "The others ran after deer, using the speed of their legs, the noses of their dogs, and a thousand well-worn tricks to bring them within reach, and often enough, the animal escaped them. . . . But the deer that Fionn got the track of did not get away, and it seemed even that the animals sought him, so many did he catch." But once again he is recognized.

"If Uail, the son of Baiscne, has a son," said the king, "you would surely be that son."

It is too early yet for Fionn to meet his destiny in the shape of the sons of Morna, and since being recognized publicly by the king makes this too likely, he departs once again, this time to the court of the King of Kerry, the man who had married his own mother after Uail's death.

Noticed immediately for his gifts, Fionn becomes a favorite companion of this new lord, and spends much time at his side. But one day after Fionn had impolitically defeated the king at chess for the seventh time in a row (no mean feat, the story implies), the king said, "Who are you anyway, by God!" and standing up from the chessboard, stared down intently into Fionn's face. Seeing Fionn so closely for the first time, he recognized, to his shock, the features of his own wife mirrored back to him. "You are the son that Muirne, my wife, bore, to Uail Mac Baiscne. You will not stay here and be killed by the sons of Morna while you are under my protection."

This sometimes instinctual, sometimes forced

moving on by Fionn is what Joseph Campbell called "the refusal of the call" either through fear of the destiny that beckons or through a deeper intuition preventing us from stepping out prematurely. Often the recognition of our gifts when too young can be too much of a burden for innocence to carry. We simply are not ready. Many would-be mentors have been encouraged by the natural gifts they see in a young protégé, only to be rebuffed because of this unarticulated but instinctual knowledge on the part of the protégé that the time is not right. In other cases, those in positions of power know that their pond is too small to hold their young student—their talents stand too far above their peers. Their talents will be wasted if they reveal themselves, and the others in the office may "kill" them if they stay.

THE SALMON OF KNOWLEDGE

"All desires save one are fleeting," James Stephens says at this point in a version of the story, "but that one lasts forever. . . . Fionn, with all desires, had the lasting one, for he would go anywhere and forsake anything for wisdom." It was in search of this wisdom that Fionn went to the place where the druid-seer Fionngas lived beside a deep pool near Slane. There he hoped to move from Call's initiations into warriorhood into the deeper understandings represented by the easy onward flow of water, and, he hoped, Fionngas's knowledge of that flow.

Arriving at the pool, he does not know that Fionngas, or Fionn the Seer, has been attempting to catch, for seven long years, the mythical and priceless Salmon of Knowledge. Being one of the greatest scholars in Ireland, Fionn the Seer has studied the ancient stories and tracked this salmon in secret, to this very pool on the banks of the Boyne River. There is an old prophesy that the Salmon of Knowledge will be caught by a man named Fionn, and that whoever eats of that salmon will become the greatest poet in Ireland, and have the gift of the second sight. The gift of intuition would have been something, but to the Irish, nothing could be of greater honor than to be the greatest poet in the land.

In ancient Ireland there was a saying, "Three equals: a king, a harper, and a poet." To understand this, we must remember that in Gaelic Ireland, a fully fledged poet, or *ollum*, had studied his art for twenty-one years. He not only knew the whole lineage and history of his people in poetic form, but had been trained to step in at crucial times of difficulty and through extemporaneous speech bring sense and clarity to the confusion of the moment, and through that give the people some sense of their beckoning collective future. In a real sense, then, the poet brought together past, present, and future in one utterance. His responsibilities were great and his place in society honored. Imagine, then, the sheer liquid ambition bursting out of the phrase *the greatest poet in Ireland.*

By means of many cunning traps, and long patience, after seven years Fionn the Seer catches the Salmon of Knowledge at last. In a fever of anticipation he builds a fire and sets up a spit to cook the fish. This is the Salmon of Knowledge and Fionngas knows it must be cooked exactly right, not too much and not too little. The fire must be of an exact temperature, not too hot and not too cool, it must be just right. He says a prayer over the fish, spits it with exquisite care along its full length, and slowly begins to turn it over the hot coals. In a welter of concentration he watches the fish begin to cook, just as it should.

The seer is almost beside himself with joy at his good fortune. He turns the fish carefully for a good while, when suddenly, looking down, he notices that the coals are getting low and the fire, if left to itself, will go out. In his excitement (and, he had to admit, his greed) he had not gathered enough dry sticks. But he cannot leave the fish to get more wood! If he stops turning the salmon on its spit, it will burn on one side by the time he returns with more fuel. If he takes the fish off the spit, the exquisite cooking process needed in order to eat the Salmon of Knowledge will be ruined. What will he do?

Normally an even-tempered and wise man, the seer is almost beside himself with anxiety when, at that very moment, into the clearing by the pool steps

Fionn, who, enchanted by the spring day and the birdsong, has almost forgotten the reason for his coming. He wanders into the water meadow so entranced by the beauty of the place that he hardly notices the older man by his fire.

"Boy, over here, what a feast for the eyes you are! Here, I'll give you a silver penny, now turn this spit. Like this, not too slow and not too fast. That's right, like that. The consequences, my boy, of burning this salmon are *terrible*. Now, my boy, look me in the eye and *swear* by all that's true that you will not eat one morsel of this salmon while I am away getting the dry wood. Swear now, not *one* morsel."

"I swear sir, by all that's true."

The seer left Fionn in the clearing, turning the spit slowly, fearful of burning the salmon by being a hair off in the speed of rotating the spit. But being the young fellow that he was, he suddenly began to smell the spring air again and listen to the cry of the hawks circling above the trees. The slight breeze in the fresh leaves mesmerized him and the spit began to turn more slowly in his hand. As Fionn's mouth dropped open in praise and wonder at the beauty of the day, the hand stopped moving altogether. Minutes later Fionn looked down and started in horror. On the underside of the Salmon of Knowledge, a blister the size of his thumb had risen in the heat from the remaining coals. "Oh, my God," said Fionn, "he'll have my guts for garters."

Being young, he did what we have all done at one time or another—he turned the spit even faster, hoping the blister would grow smaller and go away. But it did not. Now the young Fionn was beside himself. If only he could push the blister down, flatten it back into the skin, perhaps the old man might not notice on his return? He pushed his thumb gently but firmly against the blistered skin. But no! The skin broke, and three red-hot drops of salmon oil fell from the fish, onto Fionn's thumb.

With a cry of pain Fionn put his thumb into his mouth to cool it from the scalding oil, and at that very moment Fionn the Seer returned with an armful of wood. He looked into the young boy's eyes and knew immediately, seeing his eyes, that the young boy had tasted of the Salmon of Knowledge.

"What is your name, boy," said the older man. "I am Fionn, son of Uail, son of Baiscne," said Fionn slowly, but with the sheer grace that a poet commands.

"Ah," said the seer with compassionate grace, "so you are, *you* are the Fionn who was destined to eat the salmon from the beginning, and gain its knowledge as the prophesy foretold."

And *that* is how Fionn became the greatest poet in Ireland.

KNOWING BOTH:
THE SOUL AND STRATEGY

The strategic side of the mind, represented by age and experience, plans its life accordingly; it gathers knowledge, it uses cunning and tactics. It can also, at its best, wait patiently and endure hardship for a noble cause. But at the crucial moment, just as it is ready to gather its just reward, the older, experienced side of us will watch helplessly as the eternally innocent and inexperienced young fool, blessed by the grace of luck and youth, simply in the right place at the right time, wanders innocently into the clearing and takes the treasure for which we have worked so hard.

We can see this happen in outer life when a career man or woman in middle age watches someone new, younger, and inexperienced take the rewards for which he or she has worked long years, but it is also a perfect description of the soul's relationship to the personality. The soul, forever young, outlives the waning vitality of the personality bound by experience.

There is something even more disturbing about this inner relationship between the outer layer of conscious ambition and inner realm of unconscious desire; our personalities can work all the hours God sends to no avail, pushing water upstream on a project which is destined to die no matter what we do. The unawakened yet youthful soul is so entangled with the world and so physically alert, even in unconscious ways, to the tug of its own future that it does not need to keep track of every detail in order to find its way in the world.

This is not to say that we do not need the strategic

mind in the shape of the older Fionn. The point is that the salmon has to be caught, by hook or by crook, and this is exactly what the strategic mind is for. But for many of us late in our careers, by the time we get to a final savoring and consummation of the act of living, we have so neglected the young innocent inside us that there is no one left to wander into the clearing at the crucial moment, no one to enjoy the precious fruit of our labors. The glittering treasures lie like lead in our hands.

WANDERING INTO THE CLEARING

I remember my own humbling experience of the power of innocence soon after graduating from college in the mid-seventies with a degree in marine zoology, the culmination of a long dream and the beginning of my own new career in the adult world of work. Unfortunately, it was also a culmination for a whole generation of my peers. The market was flooded with life-science graduates. I suddenly realized that all these thousands of new and competitive graduates had grown up watching the same intoxicating Jacques Cousteau television programs as I had, and were now imbibing, as I was, what little oxygen was left in the job market.

Our collective dreams of sailing in the South Seas aboard the research vessel *Calypso*, following the life-style of the dolphin, were to be dashed. There were simply not enough *Calypsos* (and, judging by the number of graduates, not even enough dolphins) to go around.

In the intensive weeks before my final examinations, I remember waking from my afternoon nap in the zoology library one day (a daily experience), having worked the morning and probably most of the previous night. There before me, as I rubbed my eyes, was the latest edition of *Nature*, the most prestigious life-science journal in Britain, opened to a picture of a marvelous three-masted sailing schooner, beneath which lay an advertisement asking biology graduates to apply for the position of naturalist guide in the Galápagos Islands.

In the field of biology there is no more sacred ground than the Galápagos Islands. Here, undisturbed by human presence until the last few fleeting centuries, animals and birds have evolved in astonishingly peculiar ways and without fear of human beings. Since Darwin's voyage on the *Beagle* to those Pacific Islands and his subsequent development of the theory of evolution, it had become a kind of religious Mecca for biologists. To be a naturalist in the Galápagos Islands was, in effect, the life-science equivalent of becoming the greatest poet in Ireland.

I remember muttering darkly to myself that "there are surely five hundred people applying for that job" and I put the magazine, not without a last look of longing, to the side. To this day I still have no idea who put it before me as I dozed.

A few nights later, near the witching hour, in the study room of the small Welsh cottage where I lived, I was once more at the limit of my studying capacity. I decided that the best way to quit my books at such an early hour and rest easy in my mind, was to go and disturb *someone else* who should be studying hard. I walked through the rainy streets of the small dark village and called on a friend who, I was sure, would be burning the midnight oil. She *was* burning the midnight oil, but her resolve was stronger than mine and she refused to be disturbed. Remaining at her desk, she shouted directions for kettle and tea and told me to sit down by the fire. There in the grate was a blazing coal fire, and on the coffee table directly in front of the fire an application form. I sat down and picked up the form. To my astonishment, blazoned across the top were the words *Guides for Galápagos*. (I had just wandered into the clearing.) Another shouted conversation followed. "Are you going to apply?" "No," she called from the other room, "I decided two years in South America would be too much for me." "I see," I shouted back, "mind if I fill it in myself?"

One month later I was sitting in an old seventeenth-century inn in the small Kentish port town of Faversham, one of ninety interviewees out of five hundred applicants being seen over a period of three days. There were two positions available as naturalist guides. A veritable choir of hopeful dreamers about to be reduced to a mere duet.

The interview was conducted in an inimitable and eccentric British fashion which to this day remains in my memory as clear as the day it happened. To begin with, the applicant crowd of mostly poverty-stricken students was ushered into a large dining room and given a three-course meal complete with wine. Immediately following, we moved en mass into the bar, where we were given chits that to our amazement allowed us to order whatever we liked.

Put a large crowd of British people with a beer in their hands into a publike atmosphere, and the rest of the world can disappear. Very shortly it did. Within fifteen minutes the gentle lunchtime noise level had risen to that of a boisterous Saturday night, and people were quaffing their free pints of beer with enthusiasm.

By sheer good fortune I was in deep conversation with one of the interviewers on one of my favorite subjects—scuba diving. So engrossed were we that I hardly touched my beer. I do remember wondering vaguely on what principles they were going to make an informed choice, our abilities at conversation? The dashing figures we cut propped against a bar? Forty-five minutes into this idyllic sojourn, a bell rang, and Peter, the organizing mastermind behind this peculiar state of affairs, complete in sailor's cap and rakish cravat, stood up on a chair and announced to the horrified company that though he was *sure* we were all enjoying ourselves, he did *rather* want to start the *three-hour written examination* and see if there was anyone among us who might be appropriate for the job.

I still remember the awed and slightly stunned silence that engulfed everyone as we filed out to the waiting papers, and I said my equivalent of three Hail Marys for my narrow escape from the evils of drink, which in my student days was, I have to say, an uncommon feat. I climbed the stairs soberly aware of the befuddled and tipsy consternation that surrounded me. What were they trying to do? Filter out those with a potential for alcoholism whilst marooned in those far-flung islands?

My good luck continued with the examination. The first question involved a list of ninety boat passengers, all with their preferences for a day of sailing, with three days to fit them in. Obviously an adaptation of the same problem they had been presented by the ninety accepted interviewees for the job. My research at that time included the use of a tool called a frequency diagram. I simply poured all the names and preferences into the diagram and out popped all the passengers accommodated to their preferences. As the resolution appeared, I remember giving a startled little laugh of triumph that unnerved those around me, now working so quietly in the funereal atmosphere that had descended on the examination room.

The strange and beneficial spell that had been cast

over my appearance in Faversham continued. In the face-to-face interview that followed, I was shocked to find that all the extracurricular activities I had pursued in the face of and despite my academic workload were the very thing they were looking for.

Did I speak any foreign languages? Well, yes, I had been wasting no amount of precious time vagabonding around Europe during my vacations and picked up a little French, German, and Greek. Did I dive, well, yes, despite the horror expressed by my marine biology lecturers at the prospect of getting wet and actually going down *beneath* the sea, I was the very fanatic of a diver. My safety with the groups I would be leading? Since my early teens I had burned off days of precious study time in the pursuit of rock climbing. As a member of the university mountaineering club, I loved to introduce new members to the sport and see to their safety. So it went on.

If I have had any moment in my life when the three drops of salmon oil burned into my thumb and I tasted a modicum of its knowledge in a single involuntary movement, it was in the very middle of that interview. I knew intuitively that I had the job and felt a strange exaltation mixed with sadness at the small faith I had shown for my own desires and longings. Anyone looking from the outside might have thought that I had always followed my own wants and desires. But the essential realization that these wants and desires were central to my destiny had been missing in a truly conscious way. It filled me with a strange mixture of revelation and shame that I had not truly believed in them and that in my pursuit of what I loved I had always had the feeling of stealing time.

That was the burning part, I suppose, the three red-hot drops of salmon oil. The newfound knowledge was in the realization that everything I needed for this outrageous step into a new life, including my innocent and childlike emulation of Jacques Cousteau, I had done out of a kind of sheer joy. It was exactly what I loved most that qualified me for my next step. I felt at that moment an almost physical visitation of resolve. I remember looking out of the window of the interview room, past my interrogators and into the beautiful waters of the narrow harbor, determined never to lose faith in those personal passions and desires that had led me to this oddly miraculous place of fulfillment.

My older interior Fionn had in effect done all the hard work of catching the salmon, slogging through the hours of biochemistry, anatomy, and species identification that would get my degree. He had even figured out the railway timetable that would get me to the interview in Faversham and sweet-talked my sceptical bank manager into an overdraft that would cover my travel expenses. At the last moment of consummation, however, it was the young Fionn, somehow against all the odds, still alive within me, that had wandered in, burned his fingers, and carried off the prize.

In the Irish tradition, Tir-na-n'og, the land of the young, is the journey of a single step. Just through the gap in the edge, just the other side of the bank of mist. But it takes a lifetime to put yourself in the place from where it is *only* that single step.

The most dangerous time for a male, in his whole life, is around nine o'clock on Monday morning and then the few months following his retirement from work. This is the time of life when most severe illnesses, heart attacks, and fatalities occur. One is a death caused by the strain of carrying the burden, the other is an inability to live without the burden. A man by this time may be so involved in the strategic side of himself that he feels as if his life is over when his older interior Fionn is no longer needed in the same way.

Looking toward old age, William Butler Yeats intuited this fatal possibility in his poem "Sailing to Byzantium." The thought of a selfish old age, where his natural energies would no longer be available, and his sole focus, the size of his retirement fund, was a fate he wished to avoid.

> An aged man is but a paltry thing,
> A tattered coat upon a stick, unless
> Soul clap its hands and sing, and louder sing . . .

But long neglected, by the time of a man or woman's late maturity, the young Fionn may have died long before. Perhaps he could not shout out his lineage of blood-remembrance at the crucial moment, perhaps he was waylaid and strangled by other, more fearful aspects of the psyche, which saw him as a threat to their ordered life.

There is another side to this coin for many of the sixties generation who choose to live outside of mainstream society and stayed there. Having refused to enter into the organizational world in the first place, business, academic, or otherwise, they may have rejected structure of any kind, so that the young Fionn was kept alive but the elder Fionn was rejected. Young Fionn wandered into hundreds of clearings, but the salmon had never been caught for him to taste.

The point is to make an equal place in the psyche for both strategy and soul. We might wish to call the younger Fionn the soul side, because it is the side we have most neglected, but essentially the soul is represented by the moment of Fionn's enlightenment. His breakthrough comes through the meeting of two parts that have previously been split—our vital innocence and our knowing experience.

The story is clear, however, that it is the younger Fionn who eats of the Salmon of Knowledge in the end. We can make the intellectual and strategic side of ourselves as balanced, moral, and ethical as possible, and it is still not its destiny to experience life at its fullest possibility.

Anyone who has worked for long in a modern corporation knows that it is this younger, more innocent, but vital side of our self that is repressed and sometimes strangled by that world. The mythic realities played out in the story of Fionn tell us not to try to eliminate the strategic side of the culprit. We are the culprit. We refuse the possibility of bringing our innocence and experience together into one whole. The very act of choosing between them impoverishes our possibilities for fulfillment.

Banishing our innocence in the name of safety and good sense, we find that our capacity for vitality and enthusiasm is lost. Irrespective of our identity or our work, there are enormous interior areas inside each of us that refuse the safety that is offered by power and position and long for the freshness of firsthand experience. These are the parts represented by Fionn and his marvelous, distracted, and entangled presence in the terrible beauty of the world.

If we allow this part to emerge only outside of work, or on snatched vacations, then we are refusing the opportunity for fulfillment in the very place where we expend most of our energies, the workplace. But the story of Fionn says that this is not enough. To the soul, nothing else but our vital innocence will ever be enough. There is a destiny beckoning to be lived, and no one else can live it in our stead.

6

Taking the Homeward Road

The Soul at Midlife

W hatever graceful tension we have achieved between innocence and experience, midlife seems to come upon us unawares. The subtle changes engendered in the body, suddenly by the mirror's light, seem to be anything *but* subtle. Our mind and our heart also change radically. The world appears differently to us than it did, even, perhaps, a few short years before. No matter our surroundings, no matter our product, profit, or place in the company. Even as we reach the height of our powers, the whole weight of our existence shifts on its axis.

The business and *busyness* of the world continue around us but fade to a whispering background. The presenter continues his silent and slow-motion choreographies at the front of the room, following the red sales line with his pointer like a medieval magician, trying to capture the immense sea with a single spell. But we, looking as if from afar, stare straight ahead, and discover with a little shock that we have nothing of the old enthusiasm for all this, nor can we grant it the same life-or-death importance.

There may also be another deeper emotion coming to light, an almost pleasurable gleam of wickedness, that we have earned some kind of right through our blood and sweat to have less interest. We look but do not care to perceive, as if seeing through a glass darkly. Feeling the tide of interest and enthusiasm recede, we are not yet sure what is taking its place; something, we are sure, is happening, we just cannot seem to articulate it.

From the outside we appear as competent as ever. Each morning we pull on our shoes one after the other. We know how to do our work. We greet the others as we swing through the office door. We pull our seat close up to the desk and lay our finger purposefully on the voice-mail button. Inside us, other messages are being recorded in a language we are only beginning to comprehend. Things carry on as if nothing has happened. People at work speak to us as if nothing has changed; inside we feel solid ground giving way beneath our feet. "As if," in the poet Rilke's words, "standing on fishes."

Once, there was a shopkeeper. He had a good business in a small town some time ago in Italy. He had a wife and he had three sons. But one morning on his thirtieth birthday he went to open the door of his shop and found a corpse on the doorstep.

Stories pass one to another. I heard this shocking story first from the anthropologist Angeles Arrien. She got it from Allen Chinen's book of stories *Once*

Upon a Midlife, he got it from the Italian story collector Italo Calvino. Calvino may have heard it out of an old woman's mouth in the wilds of Italy. One day, someone years from now may say they heard this from you. Fittingly for this chapter, all good stories outlive their tellers. This is my own version of the tale.

One day, about thirty years old, we realize that there is a corpse lying across the doorway to the office. No one else is aware yet that it is there. We freeze. We look down uneasily, we *know* we had something to do with it, but we can't quite recall the circumstances.

The man was frightened. He knew he would be accused of the murder. Before he knew what he was doing, he had turned on his heels, he was off running through the woods on the outside of town. He hadn't been there since he was a boy. He took off over the hills to the great road that led off into the wide world.

Sooner or later we come across a seemingly insurmountable barrier across the path and recognize our own lifeless body. We have no desire to face this prospect at this stage in life. We flee.

Having discovered a capacity for cowardice in the face of their own destiny, a refusal to live the life that has beckoned them, a man or woman wake up one morning to find this other lost life across their doorstep like a corpse. The grief is too much. From their late twenties up until thirty-five, the youthful slayer of dragons is gone and the older wise one is yet to appear. They run.

I remember an early Sunday morning in my late twenties, driving in a strange city. I misjudged a corner slightly, and ran straight into the parked rear end of a highly polished, very expensive BMW. Before I knew what I was doing, I was down that deserted, witness-free road at high speed, suddenly panicked by the image of that immaculate taillight caving in before my dirt-cheap-car-rental bumper. I pulled over to a side street, took a moment to recover, astonished and disappointed by my cowardly reflex, and drove back to the scene of the accident to get out and leave a note of confession. Too late. The car was gone. Someone was driving home, cursing the human race and the latent selfishness lying like a curse at the center of human action.

It may be that at the first door to midlife we are finally prepared to face our own capacity for evil under duress. On the scale of things, the damaged car is very small potatoes, but what else in relationship or community have I damaged and instinctively fled from? How many invisible dead bodies lie at my door? At twenty we make a mistake, hurt people, and resolve to change our actions. After thirty we hurt a person and face again that part of us seemingly impervious to any change.

This man was lucky. He took a job as a servant in a faraway city. His master happened to be a wise man who had taken

*the name of Solomon. Every day people came to the house,
asked Solomon for advice, and paid him handsomely for the
pleasure. The man worked as Solomon's servant hard and
well for many years and did not once ask for his wages.*

We sign up and serve somebody or something. Hopefully wiser, like Solomon, than ourselves. We don't
mind if that something or someone owns us so long
as they grant us the immunity for which we long.

Be it for corporation, institution, academy or
army, we apprentice ourselves to something seemingly greater, wealthier, older and much more knowledgeable than ourselves. Our security gains us time
and space until we can ground ourselves more solidly
into our own identity. But at midlife, a man or
woman feels an inner siren call like an old memory.
No matter how long and how faithfully we have
served, we suddenly remember our former intuitions
for a possible life.

For only a moment we turn our face away from
our real desire in life because through our neglect it
has assumed the image of a corpse. Before we can
look back again, we find ourselves in strange cities
and strange hotel rooms, serving others faithfully but
neglecting the things most precious to our own way
forward. Around fifty years old we twitch the curtains
of the airport-hotel window and recognize no landscape we would willingly choose to inhabit.

Finally the memory becomes too much. We realize we have to do something about this intuition of
a better life or die ourselves, probably at our desks,

slumped over our computer screens. Trying to ignore
this physical inner pull, we may replicate our prepro-
grammed life by bonding ourselves to the actual machine. Late at night, in a high corporate tower, we
find ourselves crouched over the glowing monitor like
some ancient necromancer, leaning over the misted
cauldron of spreadsheet figures, entranced and imprisoned over long years by numerical spells we have
cast and woven ourselves.

Finally this man could bear it no longer. He told Solomon
that he must leave and return home. He asked him for his
wages for the whole twenty years and said he would depart
in the morning. Solomon was glad for him and gave him
three hundred crowns, a great sum, for all his years of
good service.

We might say that the man asked for early retirement.
Many who leave work prematurely after a lifetime of
toil have no idea how to spend their later years. Time
stretches before them like a desert. They suffer a form
of deep amnesia compounded by the neglect of their
own instincts. They have forgotten what path to take
and how to proceed. The retirement money and its
investment suddenly becomes their whole universe.

It is instructive, too, that the man wants to return
at last to his wife and family. The old, close, and intimate bonds he may have neglected while he served
out in the world suddenly reveal themselves to be the
most important ties he has. Is it too late? It may in-

deed be too late, but now it is too important not to find out. He makes for the door.

But just as the man was about to leave, Solomon asked him if, after all these years, he was going to leave without hearing a word of advice from his master? After all, hadn't he been showing people into the house for this very purpose the past twenty years? After a moment's thought, and not wanting to offend his former master, the man agreed and asked for his counsel.

"Ah, good, I have three pieces of advice for you, my good man, and you can have them for my usual fee!" *The former servant blanched but felt cornered by propriety and his own trained instincts to please his employer.*

"Go ahead, my good master, give me the three pieces of advice."

"First of all," *said Solomon, pausing for good effect.* "You are listening, aren't you?"

"Yes, I am," *said the servant.* "I am listening."

"Good, good, good," *said Solomon.* "Now give me one hundred of those crowns for the first exquisite jewel of wisdom. Thank you. First and foremost, my advice is this: Don't leave the old road home for a new one. Go back by the way you came."

"My God," *said the servant, losing his composure.* "I gave you a hundred crowns for this? 'Don't leave the old road home for a new one?'"

"You did indeed," *said Solomon.* "And you'll remember all the better for having paid!"

"What is the second piece of advice?" *said the servant,*

bracing himself to pay again and dropping a further hundred crowns into Solomon's outstretched hand.

"Don't meddle in other people's affairs. Leave other people to their own lives."

"Don't meddle in other people's affairs! I could have heard this from any second-rate fortune-teller for a hundredth of the cost!"

"Ah," said Solomon, "but at this price you will remember it!"

Under his breath and to himself, the servant gasped, "Will I now!"

"And the third piece of advice?" said the servant wearily, by now beginning to bow to his fate.

"The third piece, my friend?" asked Solomon innocently while he gracefully received and pocketed his faithful servant's last hundred crowns. "The third and last piece of advice I give to you, my long-suffering servant, is this: Save your anger until the following day."

The servant strangled a cry of indignation and repeated in disbelief. "Save my anger until the following day." The eighteenth-century Italian equivalent of "give me a break" hovering not far from his lips, he raised his eyes to the ceiling and turned as if to go.

But Solomon raised his hand and said, "But, but, but, I can't let you go empty-handed. Here, my good man, is a cake, take it and share it with your family when you reach them . . . by way of a little homecoming celebration."

The servant placed the heavy box containing the cake in his pack without pausing to look at it, called on his long years of dedication to the art of service, bit his lip, and thanked Solomon. Inside, he was seething. "Twenty years for this?" he said to himself. "Twenty years for this!"

The temptation is to look for a new road to explore. To go out again and leave what is essential behind, looking for something that lies at our own feet. Outwardly, at this stage of life, going off on new adventures, if those adventures do not build on what has gone before, may be a way of not taking up our destiny, of going to sleep again. Solomon wants to forestall this loss of identity; he wants to wake the man up and bring him back to life. He gives the servant what seem to be only clichés, but strangely, he wants him to remember what he says.

Our former servant and shopkeeper left Solomon's house half angered and half bemused by his three gems of wisdom, and as poor as he had entered it all those years before. He wasn't long on the road home before he met, like the young Fionn, a band of young and happy travelers. The man's spirits soon rose in their company. Along the road there was good talk and stories, and music and song at night in the inns. He really felt as if he had made the right decision to leave. But soon they came to a fork in the road, where his fellow travelers had their hearts set on a rough track up the mountainside. A night's detour to a village inn high in the mountains was suggested, where there was sure to be good music and song. They made a great show of wanting the man to come with them. His mouth was almost half open, about to say "Yes, of course!" when he suddenly remembered Solomon's first admonition. "Don't leave the old road for a new one." He also remembered he had paid a lot of money for that advice, one hundred crowns! "I might just as well use the advice if I paid so much for it," he thought to himself.

"Thank you, my friends, for the invitation, but I have a

*wife and three sons waiting for me at home. I bid you
adieu."*

*He wasn't half an hour down the road, when the man
heard gunshots, shouts, screams, and the clash of weapons
from the high road his friends had taken. "My God, they've
been taken by brigands, may God bless their souls! I'd be
with them and dead too if it wasn't for Solomon. Thank the
high heavens for his sound advice, a bargain at the price, if
I say so myself!"*

"Don't leave the old road for a new one." The story is
clear that this is good advice, but it emphatically does
not mean we give up any new learning on reaching
midlife. There is a whole generation of middle-aged
managers whose members are presently on the en-
dangered species list if they attempt to go back to the
old patriarchal ways with the simple hope to do them
better. Learning, partnership, and the ability to adapt
are at the core of life at work or at home. Solomon's
advice goes to a deeper level and speaks to the central
experience of a man or woman.

By saying *"Don't leave the old road for a new one,"*
Solomon is saying we have all the experience we need
now to know what kind of life to choose. By fifty we
have a gut physical knowledge of what is right and
wrong for us. We may sign up for new courses, enter
school, get that second degree, or learn a new language, but it is all secondary to a central awareness
of what is good and nourishing for our lives.

Of course, knowing this physically and being able

to follow through on this knowing are very different things. We may have made too many Faustian bargains, by our marriage, our job, or our car payments, to feel we can do anything about it. By now we know what we should do but we feel too buried by the weight of the past, our present commitments, and the terror of that beckoning new life. The cultivation of courage becomes essential. A new life beckons back along the very road we took to arrive at our present life.

The road home in some ways is the road back into the body, a time to get to know ourselves again on an interior, almost cellular level. By now, of course, the body into which we journey is middle-aged. It does not respond so well as it used to to the physical demands of the outer world, but its goals can be more humble now, more appropriate to what our hearts know is good and soul-nourishing for us. It has learned how to rest fully into our intuitions and our basic instinctual knowledge of what is right, possible, and useful.

Which is not to say that middle age is a bland form of enlightenment where wisdom comes by right of age. As this story shows, the homeward road is a dangerous one, fraught with strange turnings. Many people, in fact, seem to experience a second puberty at midlife, in the words of a friend of mine, "as confused, debauched, and restless as they were at sixteen." But confusion, debauchery, and restlessness at midlife might be symptomatic of youth's wish to preserve itself beyond its appointed time. This is particularly evident in the metropolitan, fashion-based worship of the new and the youthful. Andy Warhol could be an icon of this second puberty; his continual need to be the latest artistic wave breaking on the beach led to a self-centered second infancy, ignorant of the vast sea of inherited experience sustaining the tide on which he rode.

We may revert to a second infancy, because as Allan Chinen points out, this phase has a poignantly tragic quality to it. We can easily recognize evil, but we now realize that some solutions lie outside of our powers. We allow ourselves to experience the tragedy and grief of witnessing harrowing events without having the power or the conceit to leap on our white charger and confront them immediately. We do not refuse risky action, but we realize that we are better to approach it one step at a time, and that the final steps may be taken by someone else, after we are gone.

Shocked and frightened, but relieved at his narrow escape, the servant went on his way. But as that day turned into evening, he began to feel uneasy. He had entered a huge and seemingly impenetrable forest. There seemed to be no end to it. The road narrowed, and he walked on in the darkness for hours, sometimes feeling his way with outstretched arms. At last he glimpsed a pale light ahead of him in the darkness. As he neared the light, he realized that it shone from a cottage window, yet there was something distinctly unwelcoming about the light. Looking at the cottage made him feel uneasy, but he had no choice. He knocked on the door.

An enormous man came to the door, his face set in a frightening grimace. Without a word he waved our traveler in and pointed at the supper table set behind him. The servant took his seat hesitantly and watched his grim host wordlessly serve him soup from a large bowl. To the visitor's amazement, they continued to eat in this silence until both their bowls were finished. Just as the tall man finished his last spoonful, the servant almost leapt out of his skin on hearing a muffled knock from beneath the floor. The huge man got up, growling to himself as he did, walked over to a corner of the room, unlocked a bolt, and lifted a trapdoor in the floor.

In the light of the single candle illuminating the room, a ragged, misshapen creature slowly emerged from the opened trapdoor. To his horror, the servant slowly recognized the shape of a blind, mistreated woman. The servant's mouth dropped open as he watched the tall man reach up to a shelf and take down a human skull. Beneath the servant's gaze he slowly ladled soup into the upturned skull. Then he turned, and inserting a straw through one of the empty eyes, he gave it to the woman. She drank it without lifting her head. As she finished, the grim host lifted up the trapdoor, grunted, and pointed down. The woman half fell, half staggered back into her subterranean prison.

In the silence that followed, the tall man turned his face to the servant and said, "What, my friend, do you think of THAT!"

"I think," said the servant, about to give the man a

tongue-lashing for his cruelty, that you"—but just as suddenly, he found himself remembering Solomon's words, "Don't meddle in other people's affairs!" He found himself saying—"that you must know what you are doing. You must have a very good reason."

"I do indeed," said his fierce host. "And you may be the first guest in a long while to survive my hospitality. That poor, misshapen creature you glimpsed was my wife; years ago she took a lover behind my back, I caught them together . . . that is his skull she uses as her soup bowl. I don't forgive . . . maybe one day I'll forget, ah!"

The servant shrank back into himself as his host rounded on him. "And what, my friend, do you think of THAT!"

"I think you did the best thing you knew how to do."

"You are a very sensible man. Anyone who disagrees with me gets their throat cut. Pure and simple. Then I bury them out back. Now, let me show you to your room."

The servant finally went to sleep, half in fear, half in relief at surviving the encounter with his host. As he lay in bed, he had repeated Solomon's advice. "Don't meddle in other people's affairs!" In the morning he hurried on his way.

There is something deeper here than being told to ignore the plight of others. Our homeward-seeking servant has finally had the privilege of meeting a part of himself locked in the cellar. In the story, this part of himself is given the shape of a woman, an interior woman unable to remain faithful to him. She is a tortured representation of his locked-up feelings and intuitions, and unable to go along with the life he has chosen, she took another lover. Afraid that this wild, unfaithful representation of the feminine will leave him, she is "kept underground." But the servant is also her jailer. In the fierce implacability of the terribly wounded male who keeps her imprisoned underground, he sees himself.

Clarissa Estes notes the pivotal period of a woman's initiation down in the cellar of her emotions, underground, as the time of *la selva subterranea*, the underground forest. Estes observes that many young women are constantly making poor bargains until they finally temper their first innocence by entering this underground world. Often their descent comes through actually seeking out a man who will literally take her power away from her and catapult her into an initiatory crisis, banishing her *below* into the very ground of her being. A man's inner feminine may take the same steps, down into the cellar, hounded by the part of him that hated the fact that she sought another lover, another life outside of the busy world of work.

At midlife, then, we find ourselves again in a black wood. We grope through the dark with our hands outstretched, trying to feel the road ahead. After stumbling in the darkness for what seems like an eternity, we come to a house that stands as a mirror to the state of our soul, a small place in the forest from which only a pale light gleams. We approach it in trepidation only to have our worst fears confirmed. The "mansion" of our soul is a poor hovel inhabited only by a fierce, heartless man guarding the entrance and a powerless woman locked in the cellar.

Over the last six years of my work with American corporations, it is astonishing to witness the discontent and longing for something beyond the daily grind in men approaching fifty. I say *men* because it seems that women approaching this age find their powers more readily, as if they are better equipped for this pivotal confrontation with the latter part of life. Perhaps this has everything to do with their close relationship to the feminine figure locked in the cellar. Once their intuition is given free rein in the outer world unburdened from entrapment, they seem to breathe the air of a newfound freedom. Men seem to have more difficulties with the intuition *itself*, as if opening to its siren call may lead them in dangerous directions, far from the Elysian fields of success.

Man or woman, the touchstone seems to be the integration of those receptive, intuitive powers grounded in a form of bodily wisdom we have loosely come to describe as *the feminine*, but which belong equally to either sex.

About fifty we are ready to awaken these deeper feminine intuitions in a fuller way. We have learned by now that a peck of our own inner bodily intuition is worth a bushel of fierce self-justifications. But man or woman, we may long ago have condemned that feminine power, and her ability to follow her own star, to the black cellar.

Through this revelation, we can clearly see the difficulty in trying to mend others whose own feminine self has been locked away for years. We have all met in the workplace malevolent characters who bear a grudge against life. Or those who carry a streak of a grudge. Try to confront them with their minor cruelties, and you are likely to be threatened yourself. They have all the rationales and all the evidence. The wound is too tender, the grief too raw, and their own sense of righteousness too strong. They have condemned part of their existence to the cellar and they will not forgive it for having hurt them so cruelly. Not only do they have that initial cruelty to face but their own cruelty laid on top of it. They must now forgive not only life but also themselves for having compounded the wrong with a greater wrong.

It is a fierce reminder to ourselves when we hear the self-righteousness in our own voice. Work almost always becomes a platform for self-righteous moralizing. So much is at stake. We have given over so much of what is precious to us to achieve our place in the power structure. Certain parts of us have been dispatched to the dungeons in order to get ahead. We may hear our own defensive aggressive stance as the annunciation of hidden crimes. There is a body hidden down below. Our servant ran across someone who had condemned his inner feminine to the cellar and to foul punishments. Stepping into the initiations of midlife, we are forced to confront the equivalent part of us that has done the selfsame thing. This time around we may be ready to face the truth of what we have hidden from the world.

The neglected imprisoned feminine, kept in the

dark, is an ancient archetype. It surfaces in the stories, dreams, and poetic imaginings of all cultures and individuals where the balance has shifted dangerously toward masculine control. Serious conflict in the boardroom or on the factory floor can lead to an immediate form of masculine power reflex, and neglects a wider, more inclusive vision. Wartime especially banishes the sensitivity of intuition to the periphery of human consciousness. Throughout the ancient ten-year conflict between the Greeks and the Trojans, Cassandra, daughter of Priam, is the only one within the city of Troy who clearly sees the calamity ahead for her fellow citizens. She has the gift of second sight, given to her by Apollo, but her voice is ignored completely.

In the myth of Apollo's gift-giving, Cassandra had promised to make love with the god if only he would grant her the sight. He duly gave her the precious gift she had requested, but as soon as she had received it, Cassandra refused to give herself to Apollo. Slighted by this injustice, Apollo ordained that though she now indeed had the gift of second sight, none should ever believe her prophecies. Neither character's actions are ethical by our lights, but this was not the point of the story; the myth depicts precisely the split that occurs between the rational and intuitive powers in the internal psyche of an individual.

Cassandra's refusal is a distinct way of saying that the woman who gives herself only to the dark bodily aspects of intuition but refuses to embrace the charms of Apollo and his clear-thinking, discriminatory light-filled presence will be condemned to the shadows of hysteria.

One view might be to say that she was simply a woman who knew her boundaries. But Cassandra refused all boundaries by refusing the discriminatory powers of Apollo. In doing so, her feminine be-ingness stretched out beyond all lines so that she could not tell where she started and the world began. There was no sacred otherness. Literally no listener. No one to hear. Those who found themselves in the presence of her emotional outbursts felt they were being taken over; they simply wanted to run a mile.

Cassandra is condemned to the cellar, but she has walked into the dark herself and closed the door behind her.

Troy, of course, was eventually destroyed, as Cassandra foretold. After the city is sacked, the Greek king, Agamemnon, takes Cassandra back to Mycenae as booty. He takes her as a prisoner, but he ignores her intuitive warnings of a disastrous homecoming, taking her dire emotional prophecies as the ravings of a hysterical woman. Agamemnon also has a body hidden in his past, that of his daughter, sacrificed ten years before to propitiate the gods as the Greek fleet was about to set sail for Troy. This returning duo, Agamemnon and Cassandra, offer a heart-rending image of a total split in the internal soul life of a person. The masculine and feminine have turned their backs on one another and marched to their prospective corners in an unconscious sulk, even as they both go to their death.

On their arrival, Agamemnon is welcomed by his wife, Clytemnestra, who, unknown to him, has taken a lover in his absence, a man called Aegisthus. She has never forgotten the sacrifice of her daughter and has nursed her hatred for Agamemnon until his return. The returning king is taken to a sumptuous bath to be cleansed after the long journey home. While he is bathing, Clytemnestra and her lover throw a fishing net over the naked body of the king and murder him in his bath. Simultaneously, Cassandra is killed on the steps of the palace by the guards.

The story of Agamemnon's and Cassandra's death is mercilessly clear on the consequences of a man taking the old road home, having killed his feminine intuition, or a woman going back as the captive of a man without having developed her own powers of discrimination.

Like the man our servant discovers holding his wife in the black cellar, Agamemnon goes home with the feminine held only as a prisoner. Though the myth said that Cassandra was cursed from the start by Apollo for refusing her promise to him. The contemporary Greek poet, Ritsos, gives the story an ironic twist. The blindness to our intuitive capacities, he says, is nearer to home. Here, he says is the real reason.

THE REAL REASON

No, it isn't that Apollo reneged on his promise
and took the conviction out of Cassandra's words by
spitting in her face

*to nullify the gift he'd granted her, thereby making her
    prophecies
useless both for her and for others—no. It's just that
nobody wants to believe the truth. And when you see
the net in your bath, you think they've gotten it out
for your fishing trip tomorrow. and neither inside you
nor outside do you hear, on the palace's marble stairs,
the dark intimation coming up with hapless
Cassandra's
    wailing.*

Trans. Edmund Keeley

No. It's just that no one wants to believe the truth.
And when you see the net in your bath, you think
they've gotten it out for your fishing trip tomorrow!
The net can take many forms. At midlife it may especially be the promises of our pension fund, or visions
of ourselves, clothed in pastel golf clothes, playing
the fairways into the sunset of our lives. As if midlife
is a simple time of preparation for retirement! A giv-
ing-up of our personal destinies and contributions as
if we had nothing more to offer future generations.
Surrendering our prospective place as an elder who
has something to offer, we may plan to live in a place
where they do not allow children. We lie there naked
while the Florida condominium salesman throws the
net over our tired bodies.

Sometimes the net is more subtle. We may suddenly find we have a greater store of past memories
than we have intuition and energy for the future. We
begin to refer back to what has been, more than what

is, or might be. We may begin this strange process of disengagement, of *retirement*, years or decades before our sixty-fifth birthday.

Though the issue here is midlife, an understanding of the way we approach retirement is crucial. Our images of retirement are so often ones of disengagement from society. Many present forms of retirement that beckon us are ritual forms of giving up. Yet historically, the contribution of the elder has always been of paramount importance to the society in which he or she grew to maturity. Midlife is *exactly* the time when we reshape ourselves toward our place in the eldership. We have just begun to glimpse exactly how to pass on what, over the years, we have taken so much trouble to learn. But even as our deeper intuitions in the shape of Cassandra are dispatched on the palace stairs, we may give ourselves over to the soporific bath of retirement, buying a convenient house next to the golf course, but in the process absenting ourselves from a younger generation that could sorely use our wisdom.

The years pass in the flick of a finger before we arrive at the eighteenth and final hole. To our consternation, we find the hole is larger than we thought, a neat rectangle, to be precise, in the form of an open grave. The headstone has our name inscribed above two columns—our net worth and our liabilities. But the real bottom line equals exactly zero, a life that gave nothing to anyone.

Some of us may escape this fate. Following Solomon's prosaic but ultimately mysterious advice, we begin to see aging not as a fearful consolidation but as a graceful way of uncovering what we have to offer by way of our experience and wisdom.

Now he was almost home. He began to recognize the sights and sounds and places he knew as a boy. He hurried through the woods down the path along which he had fled twenty years before. Now, instead of fear in his heart, he had joy. He was almost there in the bosom of his beloved family. But even as he hurried, the light was failing and the shadows began to deepen as he emerged from the woodland path at the village edge. By the time he had walked up the muddy deserted street of his village, it was dark. Through the well-lit window of his former home he looked in at the family he had abandoned so long ago.

He recognized his wife immediately. She had grown older, but she had so much of the beauty he remembered. Tears filled his eyes as he gazed in from the outer darkness. Through his tears he suddenly realized that his former home was filled with people. There seemed to be some kind of celebration taking place. He heard music, saw people taking their places for a dance, and saw his wife rise to join them. To his horror, he saw a younger man also rise and embrace her. Everyone in the room applauded as they kissed, the music started, and they began to dance, embracing and laughing as they twirled around the room.

The servant was beside himself with anger. All right, he had been away for twenty years, but, my God! With another man! Right before my eyes! I'll kill him! I'll kill her! His hand instinctively reached for his dagger. He pulled it out of his belt and held it before his eyes, pointing it toward the lighted window, at the heart of the man dancing with his wife. Now, he said, prepare to meet thy fate! At that very moment, out of nowhere, he heard Solomon's final piece of advice: "Save your anger until the following day!" Hearing that, he hesitated and his hand shook. It took every last drop of his strength and willpower to sheath the dagger once more in his belt.

"Save my anger until the following day. I will, then. But then I'll kill the bastard tomorrow." And he ran off into the woods and spent a fitful night under the trees, determined to enter his house in the morning and satisfy his honor.

He did not fall asleep until just before dawn, but he woke again just after the sun had risen. Brushing himself down, he started once more up the muddy street. He hadn't gone more than a few hundred yards, when he came across an old neighbor and friend.

"I don't believe it," said the neighbor, embracing him. "After all these years, you return now, even as your son has just celebrated his ordination as a priest. His mother was so happy, she could have burst! She danced half the night with him."

"Oh, my God!" said the servant. "That's who the man was. I could have killed my own son and wife and been miserable to the end of my days! Solomon must be the wisest man I have ever met! He shook the hand of his neighbor and hurried up the street to his former home. When the door opened, there was a profound moment of silence and incomprehension followed by shouts of joy and welcome. Despite his absence, he was swept back into the bosom of his family, everyone talking at once and scouring the house for food for the celebration.

"Wait!" said the servant. "Here in my bag. A gift from my former master. A cake! He reached in and pulled the heavy cake box out of the bag. They placed the box on the table and gathered around it. The servant pulled out his dagger and flourished it above the cake. He cut down into the cake and pulled out the first slice. As he did so, gold coins began to roll out all over the table and onto the floor. When the astonishment had subsided, they counted the gold. It was the true worth of Solomon's gift. Three hundred crowns, and not a penny less!

It may be that midlife is essentially a time of remembering what is most essential to us. We have spent years building and consolidating—a business, a career, a family. Or we have attempted the same and failed to build anything. At the cusp of midlife, irrespective of success or failure, we now want to find out who was at the center of this attempt and what we were building for.

Taking the old road back home, we come across the ghost of our younger self setting out, almost fleeing, to an unknown destination, the very person who did all the work but who refused to face the corpse across the doorstep. We meet him in passing as if he were a stranger. We want to stop him, ask why he is going so far away, why he is leaving so much, but he walks through us like the spirit of the past he is.

Around fifty, we have the possibility of taking the homeward road all the way back, through the ghostly bodies to greet ourselves at our own door, before we set out. There we may welcome all parts of ourselves to the table in celebration. Here is the Nobel Prize–winning poet Derek Walcott as he approached his late forties, turning toward himself with the grace of a hard-won, mature acceptance. Taken from his book *Sea Grapes*, the first lines are clear, simple, and marvelously compassionate. The poem is titled "Love After Love."

> *The time will come*
> *when, with elation,*
> *you will greet yourself arriving*
> *at your own door, in your own mirror,*
> *and each will smile at the other's welcome,*
>
> *and say, sit here. Eat.*
> *You will love again the stranger who was yourself.*
> *Give wine. Give bread. Give back your heart*
> *to itself, to the stranger who has loved you*
>
> *all your life, whom you ignored*
> *for another, who knows you by heart.*
> *Take down the love letters from the bookshelf,*
>
> *the photographs, the desperate notes,*
> *peel your own image from the mirror.*
> *Sit. Feast on your life.*

Feasting on our life in this way, we can take from a table laden with nourishment. We have the possibility to invite even the parts we have long banished from home back to the table. Parts of us that have never before gotten in the car in the morning begin to accompany us through the traffic to work. Walcott says you *will* love again the stranger who was yourself, as if it has become for him a learned article of faith. It brings to mind certain lines of the Spanish poet Antonio Machado, translated exquisitely by Robert Bly.

> *Last night, as I was sleeping*
> *I dreamt—marvelous error!—*
> *that I had a beehive*
> *here inside my heart.*
> *And the golden bees*
> *were making white combs*
> *and sweet honey*
> *from my old failures.*

I remember at the very beginning of a trek in the Himalayas meeting three wandering mendicants under the dazzling might of the Nilgiri Wall, a breathtaking rampart of high peaks near the Tibetan border of Nepal. The three were barefoot and looked as if they had been walking and begging all their lives. Meeting them, I found they were three middle-class university professors from the south of India. At fifty, they had followed a popular Indian tradition and left their jobs on an extended sabbatical to follow the path of a spiritual pilgrim. In this way they could give themselves the time to reassess their lives as they moved toward a meaningful place in the eldership of their society. At the end of the year they might return to their former work or they might not; many leave their original path completely and make a new life.

Satish Kumar, an Indian friend of mine who now lives in England, did exactly the same thing in his own fiftieth year. Just a few years ago he left his busy job as a magazine editor and walked almost the whole length of Britain, visiting every conceivable form of sacred site, from ancient cathedrals to neolithic stone circles. He wove both worlds together by running his journey as a series in the magazine and still gave himself time to see things afresh.

Lifting our feet from the ground one after the other, we lift our spirits and our lives onto new bearings. Kumar is still editing, but he is now also the guiding force behind a new adult education center working with the principles of E. F. Schumacher's book *Small Is Beautiful*.

For every man and woman, midlife is a pivotal time of internal rebirth. No matter what we have accomplished or what we command, midlife calls on us to experience it in a new way, to birth ourselves into a new kind of usefulness. Returning from years of work, like the long-absent shopkeeper to his family, we know now the sacredness and soulfulness of belonging once again.

Those three mendicants had walked eight hundred miles from the south of India to visit the sacred temple at Muktinath. I had walked only three days from the nearby airstrip of Jomosom. We arrived at the gate at exactly the same moment. I had given myself the whole day to see the place and spend time drinking in the ambiance. They bowed, said a prayer, walked three times around the walls of the temple, and abruptly left. I watched them walking down that long valley toward the plains and felt for the first time the central importance of *journey* itself.

Between our first workday and our last we cover an equally incredible journey. Bruised by the trials and tribulations of the terrain, we might at times have felt barefoot ourselves. Finally reaching the height of our powers at midlife, we approach the very temple of our identity. Everything for which we have striven is represented by this place. Work becomes, as we sacrifice everything on the corporate altar, the be-all and end-all of our identity.

But how marvelous, then, at the end of long pilgrimage, to simply bow to what we have discovered, circle our accomplishment at work, and leave again, with the very minimum of fuss, turning our backs on everything to take the first steps of another long journey back toward the center of our selves, our family, and our communities. T. S. Eliot said it beautifully, growing into his own eldership. The lines are particularly poignant knowing Eliot found a final and long-postponed happiness in the marriage of his last years. The poem is about old age, but it is exactly this late age to which our midlife is a doorway and a preparation.

> *Old men ought to be explorers.*
> *Here and there does not matter*

We must be still and still moving
into another intensity
For a further union, a deeper communion
through the dark cold and the empty
        desolation.
The wave cry, the wind cry, the vast waters
Of the petrel and the porpoise. In my end
is my beginning.

                    "East Coker," Four Quartets

In youth, our soul's wish for a life and work of our own is tempered by triumph and failure. Gifted at midlife with Solomon's wisdom, we now yearn soulfully for a return to family and community in a new way, for a life that enriches others simply by our presence. Returning to the house from which we started, we bring Solomon's treasure hidden on our backs, and discover it in the very celebration of homecoming. We take the road of midlife not as the beginning of disengagement and retirement but as a newer and profounder path to meaningful work, the work of belonging in a deeper way to those people and things we have learned to love. The task of midlife is the task of finding the difficult, often dangerous road to this eldership of love. It becomes, for all of us, the road worth taking, the road back home.

Don't leave the old road for a new one!
Don't meddle in other people's affairs!
Save your anger until the following day!

Coleridge and Complexity

Facing What Is Sweet and What Is Terrible

". . . those who can most truly be accounted brave are those who best know the meaning of what is sweet in life and what is terrible, and then go out, undeterred, to meet what is to come." — PERICLES

W hatever our chronological age in the workplace, taking the homeward road to what is soulful in our lives is essentially an act of remembrance, the ability to rediscover a simple dwelling at the center of a complex world.

To remember what is good for our souls amid the complexities of corporate life, we must confront the shadows that fall over our work every day, and if there is any real shadow to the American workday, it has to be the way that we, as a country, descended from gritty but irrepressible dreamers, have created a work world that attempts to reduce us every day to mindless worker bees. In a country dedicated to the ideals of personal freedom, there has been endless opportunity to be a numberless corporate clone completely replaceable by another corporate clone. The iridescent colors of individual character are too often watered to a gray wash by slogans, wall plaques, and thoughts for the day. Other people's words may rise from our throats at the drop of a hat . . . *excellence . . . total quality management . . . number one . . .* but we struggle to remember the simple character of our own voice. It takes only a modicum of psychological savvy to admit that a corporate culture that constantly repeats the word *excellence* to itself must still have endless reservoirs of mediocrity on which to draw, and is deathly afraid of facing up to this fact. We open our mouths and too often utter the same phrases and opinions that might be said by a thousand other toilers in a thousand other companies. The gritty individuality of pioneer homesteaders, runaway slaves, and venturesome freebooters is suddenly reduced to a gimlet eye on the next prospect for promotion.

This chapter looks at the way the gritty individuality of everyday people and events continually grinds down the smooth machinery of our best hopes and plans. It is about our misplaced conceptions over the way the universe patterns and arranges itself not only around but *through* our work. This chapter places the imagination at the center of the soul's experience at work and looks at the possibility for a rested, internal simplicity amidst the gusts and squalls of our daily labors. It embraces the imagination as an important felt sense central to our creative survival, not only synthesizing the outer forces of order and chaos in the workplace, but drawing together from its wild-flying constituents the fabric of identity itself. In parallel, and as a way of understanding the relationship between the order and chaos of work, it draws on the infant science of *complexity*, a new child of mathematics and physics now beginning to reveal the simple elements that give rise to complex structures.

To look for this simplicity amid the grinding complexities of work, I take an incident from Coleridge's life that encapsulates not only that poet's awareness of the changing patterns of existence and his alert and vital imagination, but also his distressing inability to build the life he wanted out of what he saw. I choose Coleridge because of his genius, because of his tragedy, but ultimately because of his courage. Though he rarely found personal happiness, he remained curious, articulate, and a full participant to the end. As we must with our own struggles in the workplace, Coleridge had to come to terms with his own personal failings and make them his very way of being in the world, and in that central core of experience, that image of Job wrestling with his angel, he refused to lose faith.

THE STARLINGS

On the 26th of November 1799, traveling to London over a vast expanse of the Yorkshire moors, the young Coleridge gazed out of his carriage window and saw in the distance an immense flock of starlings sweep across the sky. He looked at it transfixed, as if the flock itself possessed a life beyond the possibilities of his own prodigious imagination.

"The starlings," he scribbled hurriedly into the skittering journal on his knee, "drove along like smoke . . . misty . . . without volition—now a circular area inclined in an arc—now a globe, now . . . a complete orb into an ellipse . . . and still it expands and condenses, some moments glimmering and shivering, dim and shadowy, now thickening, deepening, blackening!"

This restless, ever-moving image of the starlings haunted Coleridge for the rest of his days, as if it represented a side of reality whose existence he could not fully admit. Richard Holmes, his greatest biographer, saw it as "an image of shifting energy and imagination; a protean form or a force field, lacking fixed structure or outline; a powerful personality without a solid identity." Clearly, this was some sort of self-image for Coleridge, both stimulating in its sense of freedom, of "vast flights; and menacing in its sense of threatening chaos . . ."

Holmes' description of what Coleridge saw: "A *powerful personality without a solid identity*," might be a perfect description of the shifting, starlinglike nature of the corporate workplace. Work within a corporation, big or small, has become a continual grappling with a powerful and elemental character that continually refuses to define itself. Markets change or dry up in a moment. Our jobs are this day secure and the next in question again. A hundred different details and strategies dance before our eyes. The complexity of any situation, given urgent deadlines and communication technology, can develop like the arms of a Hindu god, its limbs blurring to a hidden and ultimately unknown music.

Coleridge hoped for a single vision with which to synthesize this chaotic dance. The source of this hope was the human imagination, "that synthetic and

magical power" which would lead to the "reconcili-
ation of opposite or discordant qualities." To Coleridge, the imagination was not simply the ability to
dream things up, but an actual sense, like hearing, or
seeing or touching. By *imagining*, by calling on the
internal images that naturally arose to meet outward
circumstances, it was possible to live vitally among
the confused eddies and swirls of everyday existence.

If we are confused by the small eddy of the universe
caught and bounded by our office cubicle, we can
look to the imagination and the new science of complexity to reveal to us the shifting boundary line between chaos and order, showing us not only a place
of danger, but a hidden touchstone of our vitality, our
creativity, and, at times, our very survival. But first
the difficulties that attend the attempt.

OUR LOVE OF ORDER

Much of our view of the world is formed from our
ideas of order. We hope, look for, and *pray* for order
and make the sign of the evil eye at any possibility of
encroaching chaos, yet the poetic tradition, and those
scientists studying complexity, see both qualities as
interwoven and interdependent. We are schooled to
see chaos as being the mirror-opposite of order and
an enemy of life, but scientists investigating complexity in nature see order and wildness dancing cheek
to cheek in a vital and necessary dance, informing

everything from the way the land branches and splits in an earthquake to the distribution of incomes in a modern economy.

But the human hope is for order out of chaos; we long to create stability, to find that place to stand which Archimedes sought so desperately, so that he could move the world with his newly discovered powers of leverage. The evolution of thought that came from Archimedes and the Greek world is perhaps our chief strategic inheritance. The singularity of Greek thought was its ability to create order. The Renaissance of medieval Europe was the rediscovery of those ancient Greek keys to the universe of order. My own education in a centuries-old north of England school was marvelous, stimulating, and classically grounded, but the final breath of an old approach about to crumble before the complexities of the postmodern world.

Looking at the universe in the pursuit only of order, we must literally squint to eliminate the ever-present disorder at the center of the system. While my physics teachers were solving linear equations of systems traveling in satisfying straight lines or clear curves, we were all participating in a form of collective amnesia. Scientists are finally admitting that these linear systems are almost always special cases and that almost everything we come across in life is nonlinear, that is, the shortest point between A and B is *not* a straight line because there almost never exists a straight line to follow in the first place. The line is an evolving path that actually changes according to the first steps we ourselves take to begin the journey. Most paths, in fact, metaphorical, literal, or mathematical, take the form of an iterative equation, an equation where the values and events it produces are continually fed back into the equation again and again, influencing any future values it may throw out. Every action, then, no matter how small, influences every future action, no matter how large. In the sciences, no one dared turn their face toward this Dionysian side of reality until the sixties and seventies, and no one dared listen to the scientists who had done so until the mid-eighties.

In a way, we were all feeding the hope that there was a place to stand, especially in the workplace, immune from all those disordered small actions that spoil our systems, while we could move and manipulate the world. As peace and quiet has retreated from the world since the wheels of the industrial revolution began to creak and rumble, this need for an insulated, almost quiescent state has magnified; we are all now unrequited pilgrims of silence, and our wish for an island of quiet is often lived out through our wish for control over others and their actions.

THE MANAGER WHO IS NOT

Part of our difficulty is that we send the same strategic part of ourselves that loves order out to embrace the disorder in the world and scare ourselves to death because the strategist, or *manager*, in us cannot deal with the terrifying revelations hidden in life's unpredictability. Life simmers for long periods and suddenly without warning comes to the boil. Markets collapse, good products don't sell, factories burn down, the wrong people are fired. The right people are suddenly promoted—to the wrong positions. A manager *manages*, but only a human soul gifted with imagination has the resilient artistry to live and work with forces that call for deeper strategies than containment.

Turbulence has always caused humans difficulty, but tie this with a corporate culture focused on managing clean results, and it assumes the image of a demon ready to trap unwary travelers on the career path. Scientists trying to quantify the headlong tumble of a mountain river or the wild unpredictability of a storm front have had equal difficulty. In James Gleick's definitive book *Chaos*, he quotes the revolutionary physicist Werner Heisenberg on his deathbed, declaring that he will have two questions for God: "Why relativity and why turbulence?" Heisenberg mused, "I really think He may have an answer to the first question."

If a divine power in the world did have anything to say on the matter of chaos, it would probably be in the form of a terrifying silence. Some truths are too difficult for human beings to bear, especially when they are trying to get a job done. Hurrying from one work station to another, we hope the hurrying itself can grant us the importance we seek. Slowing for a moment, we might open up the emptiness at the center of all form.

Managers, being true to their title, have until now unconsciously followed the second law of thermodynamics, the belief that everything in the universe tends toward disorder, unless, of course, it is *managed*. Modern "managers" might be better dropping the title of manager itself and, following the dynamics of complexity, discover in the process that natural systems tend to move toward and find their most vital form at the *boundary* between chaos and order. This vitality can be seen in the way living organisms walk with exquisite precision the almost nonexistent line between predictability and adaptability. One step too much to one side or another, and like most companies in a fast-developing market, they will not survive their particular generation. Yet an organism would certainly be caught on the side of imprisoning order were it to attempt to "micro-manage" its way through existence.

Stephen Covey has done some thinking on this matter and calls his alternative to the traditional management approach "release management." A poet might take a little time somewhere to come up with a title that "released" the word *manager* altogether, though these attempts to replace titles are fraught with difficulty. The word used as an alternative is often *coordinator*. *Coordinator* emphasizes the process of drawing together and concentration rather than the caretaking and control aspects of the word *manager*, but it is far too mechanical a description for the resilient artistry that the new workplace demands. Another attempt I remember was the word *focalizer*, one who focuses a team or community of people rather than *manages*.

Whatever the language, the only systems of management that tend to stand the test of time are adaptable ones, often ones that can grow and evolve into systems which hardly resemble their predecessors.

THE CENTER OF THE WHIRLWIND

Like Coleridge looking from his jolting carriage window, those working in corporate America today see a world forming and reforming before their very eyes. And like Coleridge, their very existence is at stake. No matter how powerful their company, the nature of our times makes most structures, especially large ones, as permanent as chaff in the wind. IBM sheds jobs in a never-ending molt. Kodak, once the imperial center of photographic reproduction, finds its old patents and processes obsolete before the oncoming digital future. Technological solutions previously undreamed are suddenly made real by competitors; the flock of competing companies divides around an obstacle and suddenly reforms into a whole again, like a living being.

As we near the end of the twentieth century, we

begin to see the settled organizational life of the fifties and sixties in some historical perspective: one of those rare periods in the evolution of a system when the elements combine to form a stable structure. Technological development was slow but steady. The number of real foreign competitors was low. Much of the world was still economically undeveloped or still in recovery from World War Two. The expanding economy provided real succor and shelter for a whole generation scarred by the Great Depression of the nineteen-thirties. God was in his heaven and all was right with the American world. All the irritations of the natural world would be removed by new technologies and the corporations that mastered them, from the elimination of insects to the guaranteed temperature of a well-needed drink.

We are less innocent now and less under the illusion of a natural American or even human supremacy. Many of those illusions have not been released without a fight, but they are all but gone. The world in many ways has turned back into the mythical kingdom our ancestors perceived for millennia.

The corporate world, for so long under a steady rotation, is now being spun ever faster by constantly changing variables; foreign competition and cheap labor threaten our jobs, faster communications give us little time for rest, and the blur of funds that cross the screens of far-flung currency speculators seem to render our individual efforts more and more marginal.

Both from a personal and corporate perspective,

the world has become once more an ever-changing, fast-moving place at once magnificent and nourishing, tawdry and dangerous. Our jobs disappear in an instant. The *industry* in which we came to maturity goes away overnight. Even the heavens and the air is changing. Just as our neolithic ancestors could not take the rising of the sun for granted, we now gaze at a sky losing its protective shield of ozone, unsure if it will continue to nourish us or become the actual source of our demise.

Our times seem to call for a full unblinking look into the dangerous face of something we once thought of only as our protector. Doing this with a measure of calm, strength, and courage, without giving in to fear and panic, may be the measure of any meaningful survival.

Looking into that future, we begin to see that we cannot split off the vitality we ardently wish for in our work from the same vitality that gives the world its awe-inspiring and destructive mutability. To meet the fiery qualities of the world, we must be able to live with a little fire in the belly ourselves. Like athletic or artistic endeavor, taking the reins of responsibility in an organization at whatever level takes some education and experience, but without a vital ability to tackle the fiery qualities of the present, neither education nor experience are of much use.

We can have fire in our approach only if our heart is in the work, and it is hard to put our heart in the work when most of what we feel is stress. The very act of slowing into our own more natural rhythms may seem like a heart-stopping prospect, but there are some elegant lessons in the very reasons a heart may stop or start.

THE RHYTHMS OF THE HEART

In terms of human vitality, medical researchers have found the presence of chaos as a basis of robust health. It has long been puzzling to physiologists that biological rhythms (such as the tireless human heartbeat), rhythms that never repeat themselves in quite the same way, are the basis of managing so many of the body's vital systems. The heart varies its rhythm and rate of blood flow with almost every movement, yet displays a remarkable consistency over time. Study living organisms and their vital regulatory systems, and it becomes apparent that completely predictive systems, given even the barest of nudges, tend to continue flying off course on a dangerous trajectory, as if their regular march is an end in itself, indifferent to the life of the system.

Watching the marching, dull and unwavering trace of a human heart on the CRT screen, a doctor finds one of the sure signs of a heart about to die. It lacks robustness. Disturb it and it will careen into complete stasis or complete chaos. A healthy heartbeat full of strange little flourishes and incongruous leaps, but true to an overall pattern over time, given the same nudge, always settles easily, disturbance over, back into a life-giving beat.

This issue of robustness seems critical: the ability of a system or person to withstand the tiny but constant slings and arrows encountered every day without being nudged into a physiological dead end. Learning of this, we surely must cry out in joy and confirmation for all the little insanities and eccentricities that inform our personal organizational systems and keep them robust and healthy. Just as critical in a living system is its flexibility, its ability to adapt to and function in a range of environments.

Being locked into a single response, we become slaves to the world as we think it should be, unable to ride with the curving undulations of existence. Plants and animals must adapt to a world that changes rapidly and unpredictably; just so the postmodern corporation, and just so a person working in that corporation. No heartbeat can be locked into the strict rhythms of simple models taught in traditional medical schools; it would be a sentence of death, just as no entrepreneur could lock their excited energy into the neat predictions or abstract models of macroeconomists.

Yet in corporate America it may be that the robust but aching human heart is the organ that carries most of the burden and pressure, and under that pressure frequently begins to fail. Looking out of our windows, gazing at the starling movement of our corporate future against the sky as if at a swirled pattern of tea leaves, we do not see any indications of a better or calmer life. Like Coleridge's starlings smoking over the ridge toward our carriage, present-day corporate America is alive with movement yet filled with dark and brooding omens. It feeds our economy, our families, and our communities, yet does as much to break apart those same communities, families, and individuals who work for it as any force we have in our society.

It is hard to *belong* to corporate America. Jeansmaker Levi Strauss, in the words of its eloquent chairman, Robert D. Haas, "buys denim in North Carolina, ships it to France, where it is sewn into jeans, launders these jeans in Belgium, and markets them in Germany, using television commercials developed in England." Levi Strauss has had to do this for good reason, to survive, yet, hearing this, we learn very quickly how expendable any one of us might be, equally exchangeable for a stranger who did not grow up with cold milk and Oreos or Little League and "The Star-Spangled Banner." Corporate America seems to encompass our whole vision yet refuses to belong or care for any one place or person. It asks us for commitment and dedication and then goes its own way, shifting its goals in order to prosper and survive, and devil, it seems, take the hindmost.

Faced with this, our hope at work may be for a quiet corner out of the mainstream rush of a world that refuses any longer to play fair. Knowing we may be left behind in the fiery rush of the company as it lifts off for another continent, the very deadness of an organization may seem like a welcome respite faced with the swift-moving nature of postmodern business. We might start to reinforce whatever pockets of conservatism we can find. We are suddenly on the defensive. We stop working at the edge between creativity and failure and start managing change in the best way we know—by attempting to diminish its occurrence. We begin to march to a regular internal beat. We begin to find ways of making ourselves invisible in the organization so that others will deal with the onrush of events. Our energies increasingly move toward a complicated and often Machiavellian rearguard action to stave off defeat. The simple innocences of creative urgency are gone and forgotten. Finally, we learn how to keep our heads down and endure, hoping the CEO's finger of death will not point to our department as things go slowly but irrevocably wrong.

The psyche of an individual or a corporation caught in this negatively reinforcing hoop of evasive action is like the first step of someone on the slippery slope to self-destruction. As if the world is suddenly now too complex to deal with and all hope of finding a place to stand has been lost. A complicated world seems to stand between us and our chosen life, demanding ever more complicated ways of being. We're tempted to nod in recognition at Salinger's character Zooey in *The Catcher in the Rye*, when he snaps: "Yes, I have an ulcer, for chrissake. This is Kaliyuga, buddy, the iron age. Anybody over sixteen without an ulcer's a goddamn spy."

"I could not simplify myself," writes the suicide in Turgenev's *Virgin Soil.* As if he had discovered the very question lying at the center of existence but could not answer it, even to save his life.

THE IMAGE AS A GATEWAY TO SIMPLICITY

We can see this soulful need to simplify as being an equally soulful need for rest. It seems representative of much of our lives that, looking at the research into sleep patterns in North America, we are most of us chronically underslept. We are burning the candle at both ends, and some of us, if we can, in the middle too. Rest, as we all know, brings perspective, vitality, and good humor. But it also brings a relaxation into inner silences and images that are sometimes too difficult to face. We might wonder if this has anything to do with our addiction to being busy. Concerning ourselves with the music of the busy outer world, we might not have to face the inner music that was composed as a score for our future destiny.

Taking time for ourselves and allowing an easy rest into the body gives permission for our deeper unconscious life to stir. Images germane to our future spontaneously begin to rise to the surface. A certain inner fire begins to burn. These images have to do with our deepest and perhaps most precious desires. We intuit the tongue is close to the articulation of these images when we feel at once a strange *and* familiar exhilaration tinged with grief, embarrassment, and often, if they have remained unspoken, regret.

The emergence of our private desire-images causes turmoil and unaccountable little leaps in the body. Yet these first tentative steps toward what the poets have called *the life of the imagination* can be disturbing. If we are not used to the plethora of variations that make up a consistent path, we may try to eliminate them and erase our possibilities for adaption in the process. One way we conspire to eliminate these little creative pirouettes is to speak about them with people who have no time for them; they help us to avoid our own path by letting us agree with their cynicism, a form of self-inflicted sabotage. But the images we have sabotaged are in Keats's words *the truth of the imagination*. We sabotage our creative possibilities because the world revealed by the imagination may not fit well with the life we have taken so much trouble to construct over the years. Faced with the pain of that distance, the distance between desire and reality, we turn just for a moment, and quickly busy ourselves. But then we must live with the consequences of turning away.

Some time ago, at AT&T, I found myself working with a roomful of particularly thoughtful managers. We were looking at the way human beings find it nec-

essary to sacrifice their own sacred desires and personal visions on the altar of work and success. Out of
this a woman wrote the following lines. She read
them slowly from the back of the room, unaware how
stricken we all were by the silence she created.

> *Ten years ago . . .*
> *I turned my face for a moment*
>
> *and it became my life.*

We have patience for everything but what is most important to us. We look at the life of our own most
central imaginings and see it beckon. For the most
part, we have not the courage to follow it, but we do
not have the courage to leave it. We turn our face for
a moment and tell ourselves we will be sure to get
back to it. When we look again, ten years have passed
and we wonder what in God's name happened to us.

> *I turned my face for a moment*
> *and it became my life.*

A poet faces the daunting task of following her star.
No one places a hand on her back and congratulates
her on her choice of profession. No one points out
the generous dental plan that goes with the job. She
falters at her future and she falters at the open page,
she hesitates, turns her face for a moment, and signs
up for three years of college English. Looking back,

she wonders now why she writes like everyone else, and why so much of her passion goes into gender-neutral language.

There is the same poetic imagination in every entrepreneur or every maverick in a structured company. We are constantly being asked to turn our faces away from our own internal images of what is right, true, and most of all *alive* for us. The very simplicity of these images may seem to speak against them. They may be images of harmonious relationship, a vital company producing useful things, a new product, a life in the country, a loving family, or clear, simple images of flames, swords, feathers, iridescent birds, or enticing forest paths. We give them away thinking they cannot be reflected by the complex experience of the world in which we have learned to live. But giving them away, we find ourselves strangely empty. Finally, we understand that though the world will never be simple, a life that honors the soul seems to have a kind of radical simplicity at the center of it.

For example, as managers faced with an overwhelming situation of complexity, we could take a step back from the situation by asking our deep psyche for an internal image to guide us through the labyrinth we face. This can be done with a minimum of fuss, simply by sitting back in our chair and closing our eyes for a moment. Having asked for an image, it can, with a little practice, appear spontaneously. The task as a poet is to make the internal image ap-

pear whole in common speech. The task in the workplace is to create the circumstances or product held
in the image. The discipline over time in both poetic
and work worlds is to make the gap between the image
and the action as slender as possible. In Japanese
Haiku written by the great practitioners, there is no
gap between image and reality. The image is the experience the moment it is uttered.

> *Scarecrow above the hillside*
> *rice fields.*
> *How unaware! How useful!*
>
> *Basho*

The image will give not only an indication of strategy,
but also tell us what way we should *be* as we navigate
the situation. It may be the image of a scarecrow asking us to drive off corporate raiders simply by our
presence. It could be the image of a bull asking us to
dig our heels in and lock horns. It could be a small
flower opening slowly in morning light, or a bird
bursting into flight, waves on a beach, or a glass
paperweight being shattered by a hammer. In this respect, as Basho would have said, first thought, best
thought!

The image can be sought internally or externally,
I remember being completely overwhelmed as the di-
rector of a residential education program in the Pacific
Northwest. Finally, pushed over the edge one day by

a small incident, I walked out into the woods surrounding the center and told myself to look for a sign
or image that would indicate a better way of dealing
with the whole stressful state of affairs. Though the
immediate image before my mind was that of a branch
from which to hang myself, I did quiet my mind
enough to recognize the teaching image when it appeared—a small bird, working its way up a decaying
cedar stump, pushing its beak without fail into every
minute hole in the stump, looking for a supper of insects. The bird did not overlook any part of that log as
it slowly, over twenty minutes, worked its way to the
top. It wasn't what I wanted to see, but it was pure gold
as far as what was needed. One step at a time, and don't
miss any of the steps, not even the smallest! One step
at a time! My sanity for the year that followed hinged
on the physical presence of that image, conjured not
only as a reminder but as *a way of being*.

It's not that we have to continually remind ourselves what the image means over time, though this
can be useful. Simply finding the place in our psyche
where the image lives tends to bring about the very
quality that the image holds for us. For instance, this
image of the bird is busy yet restful at the same time.
A discipline of calling up an image is an old form of
contemplation. But a further step is to rest into the
way the body feels in the presence of the image, then
the image can be released and the state itself reached
directly. Images, like everything else, belong to a
changing reality, and we have to be ready to let them

go when the time is right. The image is not static,
just as our struggles at work are not static.

This summoning of internal imagery may seem
like the description of miraculous oracular powers,
but it is really the simple process of uncovering something our deeper psyche already knows. The deep
psyche, or soul, left to find its way, will offer up or
recognize in the outer world the images germane to
its place on the path of life. That's it, the soul seems
to say. That's how it looks from here. That's it!

The simple internal image gives us an encapsu-
lated summary of the issues central to our lives at any
moment. Like a dream, it is astonishingly accurate at
taking the measure of our present struggles and indi-
cating the path we are on. But the important thing is
not to overinterpret the image or the dream. We place
too much burden on it if we are too quick to say it must
mean this or it must mean that. The main point is to
live with the image or the dream and let it work its
magic on us. In a meeting, for instance, when faced
with the persecutor who seems to be making our lives
miserable, we can hold our image of locking horns
in the mind's eye even as we are speaking with our
antagonist. It is extraordinary how much of the power
carried by the image itself will be present in our voice.

The image, in a sense, is much bigger than we are.
It is, as the Jungian psychologists say, *archetypal*, that
is, it has informed human life since the beginning of
time and transcends individual experience. We can
think of a few strong souls who had clear and supra-

personal inner images to guide them, Martin Luther King and his "dream" image of racial harmony. Gandhi's spinning wheel from which he slowly but miraculously spun independence for India. J. F. Kennedy's "Ask not what your country can do for you . . ." Joan of Arc's vision of France in a wheat field. Again and again, those who seem to have the qualities of soul and the images of soul for which we hunger seem to be at home with themselves; they literally have a place to return to, an inner image or reflection that they can look fully in the eye.

THE IMAGE AS A GATEWAY TO HIDDEN GRIEF

Making the first difficult, half turn of our face toward that inner reflection held by the image we have uncovered, we take an important step home. We sense the possibility of a new life in that image, but we also sense things in it that until now we have denied about ourselves. I wrote this poem, *The Half Turn of Your Face*, as if looking into a mirror, in a sobering moment of self-assessment.

> *The half turn of your face*
> *toward truth*
> *is the one movement*
> *you will not make.*

*After all
having seen it
before.*

*You wouldn't
want
to take that
path again.*

*And have to greet
yourself
as you are
and tell yourself
what it was like
to have come so far
and all in vain.*

*But most of all
to remember
how it felt again
to see
reflected
in your own mirror
the lines
of abandonment
and loss.*

*And have those words spoken
inviting you back,
the ones you used to say,
the ones you loved
when your body was young
and you trusted
everything you wanted.*

Hard to look,
but you know it has to happen
and
that it takes
only the half turn of your face
to scare yourself
to the core.
Seeing again
that strange resolve in your new reflection.

Coming to the life of the imagination, then, is both a liberating path of understanding and a fearful exercise in self-revelation. We must face not only the simple guiding images alive in our breasts, but the long years we have neglected them. They lie calmly, at the very center of the whirlwind, as if waiting for us. The simple clarity of the images themselves may seem like a taunt to the complex life now pulling us in a hundred directions. Yet in them, beneath the surface of our daily lives, we see the determination of that resolve in a deeper, newer reflection.

Rainer Maria Rilke, the great German-speaking poet whose books the Nazis burned exactly because of his faith in the internal image independent of outer controls, imagines a man looking out of his window at summer's end, having been busy with everything except the one harvest that mattered. Consumed by work, this becomes increasingly easier to do. Overwork can become a kind of amnesia from which it becomes increasingly difficult to break.

Now, already, the ripening barberries grow red,
and the old asters hardly breathe in their beds.
Whoever is not rich, now that summer goes
will wait and wait and never be themselves.

There are certain harvests that never come to us again
if they are not gathered in season. More fearfully, we
must face the part of us that may not have planted in
the first place.

The man who cannot simply close his eyes
knowing there is image after image
far inside him, waiting quietly until night
to rise around him in the embracing dark
it's all finished for him, he's just like an old man.

Those with busy lives, but bereft of the inner images
based on the soul's desires, have empty larders, and
no fire in the hearth; they will starve if they are not
fed something more nourishing. Especially if the
abundant season of fall changes to winter. I remember the story of a Jewish concert pianist, locked into
a confined space with dozens of others by the Ger-
mans. She survived by playing mentally through her
entire repertoire of Chopin while everyone died in a
standing position around her. The inner-soul images
are different for all of us. Whatever they are, if we do
not give them the ground to grow and blossom . . .

Nothing comes to greet him any more, nothing happens
all day, and even the things that do happen cheat him,

even you my God. And you are like a stone
that draws him, day by day, into your depths.

Here is Rilke's full poem:

Now, already, the ripening barberries grow red,
and the old asters barely breathe in their beds.
Whoever is not rich, now that summer goes
will wait and wait and never be themselves.

The man who cannot simply close his eyes
knowing there is image after image
far inside him, quietly waiting until night
to rise all around him in the dark
it's all finished for him, he's just like an old man.

Nothing comes to greet him any more, nothing happens
all day, and even the things that do happen cheat him,
even you my God. And you are like a stone
that draws him, day by day, into your depths.

                              Trans. David Whyte

THE IMAGE AS GATEWAY TO HEALING: THE REST BETWEEN THE NOTES

Rilke asks us to fall toward our own personal destiny, no matter what that destiny may be, to feel the natural weight of the soul's images and desires, which in the poem above he saw as the gravitational weight of God's presence, pulling us to a center of absolute silence and pure simple beingness. At that center we work because we love our work, and we love our work because we have chosen the *right* work, the work to which we belong. But Rilke does not ask us to ignore the fraught nature of the world to do this; he simply asks us to embrace it in a larger perspective. For instance, he says, imagine your life as a piece of music. But stop putting all your attention on the notes.

> *My life is not this steeply sloping hour,*
> *in which you see me hurrying.*
> *Much stands behind me; I stand before it like a*
> *   tree;*
> *I am only one of my many mouths*
> *and at that, the one that will be still the soonest.*
>
> *I am the rest between two notes,*
> *which are somehow always in discord*
> *because death's note wants to climb over—*
> *but in the dark interval, reconciled,*
> *they stay there trembling.*
>
> > *And the song goes on, beautiful.*
>
> > *Trans. Robert Bly*

The greeting card carrying a bad poem says, "life is a symphony." Looking at this, at least half of us must turn away and leave the room in order to continue reading. Life in corporate America is emphatically *not* a symphony. But notice how Rilke's internal image of music and silence has room for all parts of us to read the poem. He includes not only the triumphant notes, but the part of us that fights through the rain and traffic to work, cursing modern life.

> *I am the rest between two notes,*
> *which are somehow always in discord*
> *because death's note wants to climb over—*

These notes of discord dominate our lives,

> *but in the dark interval, reconciled,*
> *they stay there trembling.*
> *And the song goes on, beautiful.*

Rilke finds a marvelous rested simplicity by living out what we normally call "the balancing act," but he would see it more truly in terms of a vibrant tension between opposites. His life is neither the notes nor the silence between the notes, but the music that arises out of sound and silence felt as a living whole. Stop choosing, he says, between chaos and order, and live at the boundary between them, where rest and action move together. You can never eliminate the process of chaos from existence, but equally, you cannot completely cover over the calmness that lies at the center of everything. Embrace reality by embracing both. Stop choosing! All very well, we say, "but show me."

SIMPLICITY AMID COMPLEXITY: THE STRANGE CASE OF THE STRANGE ATTRACTOR

The new science of complexity, ironically, looks this question of simplicity directly in the eye. Why should it be that simple elements following simple rules will often engage in the most outrageous, hard-to-predict patterns? And how is it that simple elements will, as if guided by an unseen hand, spontaneously arrange themselves into astonishingly complex structures like mountain ranges, rain forests, planets, supernovas, or detailed, three-hundred-page reports?

The basic elemental building blocks of human aspiration are the elements of individual imagination, those particular images to which a person's inner longings and desires naturally turn to express themselves. Previously, we have left this *life of the imagination* to poets and artists. What would it be like to grow organizations whose complexity arises from the cross-pollinating visions and imaginations of their constituent members? This does not entail a Polly-anna policy of "anything goes." Given the need for a profit and certain clear ethical restraints and guidelines, why not allow people to realize these goals according to their own inner images of what is right good and true? particularly if they are members of teams or communities within an organization? Why not have faith in the complexity that arises from their interacting individual images, their imaginations?

For example, I know a team of people working in the editorial department of a large publishing company who do not have the comparatively inexpensive computer and communications technology that would simplify and enhance their work considerably. The overarching bureaucracy of their company does not seem to allow them to go out and choose what they would need to simplify time-consuming tasks at the stroke of a key. Whatever communications equipment they have is chosen for them. The bureaucracy may produce evidence in the boardroom that it has saved much money on the equipment they did buy that year, but that dead hand on the imaginations of the team is actually acting at great cost, expense, and stress to all concerned, including the authors who attempt to supply them with manuscripts.

All the evidence from the science of complexity says that given certain clear parameters, the communities or teams will become self-organizing. They will be attracted to certain flowing states of organization natural to the people who make them up. In chaos theory, these flowing states are poetically called *strange attractors*.

A strange attractor is a pattern that traces the swirling evolution of a system, say a pendulum, given slightly irregular taps in a circle. The system is chaotic because it is impossible to know exactly where the pendulum will be next, but charting the system over time, it will begin to show an overall pattern to which it returns again and again. Even the most chaotic of pendulum swings will never overstep certain boundaries; it will move within a shape that we come to recognize as the pendulum's *strange attractor.*

A work team made up of collaborating individuals would also have, if you could measure and plot creativity, failure, and success, a strange attractor that depicted the edges and patterns of the team's behavior. This pattern would be constrained by the forces operating within the company and outside in the market, but it would be most affected by the focus and vision of the team. A strong vision and purpose acts as a kind of strange attractor, allowing individual creativity while acting as a natural constraint to behavior that is detrimental to the team. Without repressive rules, then, a cohesive team with a strong sense of its mission, ethics, and tasks can be allowed a lot of leeway to develop its own approach to problems.

Strange attractors in nature were first discovered by the computer simulation of weather patterns. Here is James Gleick from his book *Chaos,* speaking of their discovery: ". . . revealed by computer exploration, the strange attractor began as a mere possibility, marking a place where many great imaginations in the twentieth century had failed to go. Soon, when scientists saw what computers had to show, it seemed like a face they had been seeing everywhere, in the music of turbulent flows or in clouds scattered like veils across the sky. Nature was constrained. Disorder was channeled, it seemed, into patterns with some common underlying theme."

Gleick also captures a marvelous rhapsody on the matter by theoretical biologist Otto Rössler. Rössler felt that these shapes (the patterns drawn by the plotting of natural strange attractors) embodied a self-organizing principle in the world. He would imagine something like a wind sock on an airfield, "an open hose with a hole in the end, and the wind forces its way in," he said. "Then the wind is trapped. Against its will, energy is doing something productive, like the devil in medieval history. The principle is that nature does something against its own will and, by self-entanglement, produces beauty."

and, by self-entanglement, produces beauty.

But what is useful in knowing about strange attractors and self-entangled beauty for those of us struggling through a self-entangled but ugly day in the office? Firstly, and most useful, the image of the strange attractor tells us that even the most entangled and chaotic of systems is made up of many orderly behaviors; it's just that none of them can ultimately dominate the larger pattern, but scientists have found that if the system is disturbed in certain ways, one of those many regular behaviors can be encouraged to emerge. Built into a chaotic system, then, is an unusual flexibility that allows it to switch quickly between many different behaviors, making it inherently adaptable and multifaceted.

Second, a strange attractor will never stray beyond certain boundaries; it will always remain held by the boundaries of its strange attractor. In other words, there is always some underlying image to look for in the chaos that will give you a key to the next level of order. Any experience of chaos, then, is an incomplete experience of a much larger, more ordered system, though in the moment we may not have the perspective or stillness to see it. By the same token we must accept the other side of the coin, that the order and calmness of a given day is simply one level of a larger, much wilder, disordered scheme of events. Embracing both these sides of experience, we stop trying to create permanent order or throw up our hands at the seemingly permanent chaos and instead start paying attention to the swirling patterns rising and disappearing before our eyes. This may sound abstract to those managers still able to operate in stable markets, but for those managers now working in the fast-moving computer industry of the nineties, this ability to see patterns emerging from the swirling intangibles of supply and demand is essential to their work and their company's survival.

Gleick is continually quoting scientists like Rössler, forced into the inspired realms of lyrical poetry in order to describe the vibrant patterns that emerge when nature itself acts under constraints. But, we may ask, we hear about beauty, I want beauty, but what if profit slips from my grasp in the intoxicating process of self-organization and self-emergence? We want beauty *and* profit. Or, remembering the title of James Autry's recent book, we might even ask for *Love and Profit*.

Autry is a former president of the Meredith Corporation, and along with Dana Gioia, one of the few good poets to emerge from the maw of corporate America in the eighties. Here is his own perspective on self-organizing principles in the workplace, quoted from an interview in *The New Paradigm in Business*:

See, the bottom line follows everything else. We say in our company that profits are like breathing, it's required. So we don't pay a hell of a lot of attention to it. What we pay attention to is creating an environment, setting up the circumstances and the goals (the strange attractor) so people can do the work that produces the bottom line. I have a little poem called "Threads," and it ends like this:

> *Listen.*
> *In every office*
> *you hear the threads*
> *of love and joy and fear and guilt,*
> *the cries for celebration and reassurance,*
> *and somehow you know that connecting those threads*
> *is what you are supposed to do*
> *and business takes care of itself.*

From a poet's point of view, Autry misses an important fiery step between threading "love and joy and fear and guilt" and "business taking care of itself." Because we all know that no matter how much we thread all these things together, businesses can and do fail. They are not the recipe for immunity that the poem implies. But it does indicate a sure knowledge on the part of Autry, after decades of successful business, that these invisible elements of connection are far more important than are generally acknowledged.

Autry goes on to say, "I wouldn't for a minute want anyone to think that's management by the wimps, or mushy, without discipline or control. It's not. It's a matter of providing the kind of environment where people exercise their own discipline and control."

As Waldrop quotes Physicist Steven Wolfram: "Whenever you looked at very complicated systems in physics or biology . . . you generally find that the basic components and the basic laws are quite simple; the complexity arises because you have a great many of these simple components interacting simultaneously. The complexity is actually in the organization—the myriad ways that the components of the system can interact."

Or returning again to Wordsworth's lines from "The Prelude," written almost two hundred years ago, quoted in the first chapter of this book:

> *There is a dark invisible workmanship*
> *that reconciles discordant elements*
> *and makes them move in one society.*

Simple elements thrown together, even at random, exhibit tremendously complex behavior. Complex behavior can suddenly give rise to simple systems, and the laws of complexity seem to hold at every level, indifferent to the elements that make up the system. A calm manager working with simple paddle strokes can ride a turbulent river of events into calm water, while a frenetic manager may be overwhelmed and drowned simply by attempting to account for every swirl and eddy of the torrent.

Like the ancient symbol of the snake eating its own tail, the complex mystery of existence is continually being devoured by the simplicity on which it rests. Examine the simplest particle of that simplicity and the jaws of the snake open again, revealing the complex patterns lying beneath simplicity itself.

In some ways Coleridge committed a form of artistic suicide attempting to solve the complicated mystery he saw in the flocking starlings. In a harrowing self-indictment he later described himself as a ". . . starling self-encaged, & always in the moult, & my whole note is, tomorrow & tomorrow & tomorrow." Slowly losing confidence in himself as a poet, he attempted to become an all-knowing philosopher-king. He ignored the simpler images central to his life as a poet and attempted to create an equally complex system of philosophy that would hold it all in place. He eventually produced the *Biographia Literaria*, an immense tome, impressive in learning, thought, and scholarship, but in my heretical opinion as unrepentant lyric poet, a tragedy of wasted effort and a loss to us all compared to the vital genius of his early poetry.

This happens in a parallel fashion to many skilled managers who convince themselves that the organization's vision is their own vision. They suddenly find themselves in positions that are seen as rewards for rather than consummations of their skill; their natural abilities may not translate into the job they have been promoted to, nor may their interest, but because of the pressures of the career path, they may convince themselves into a phantom life under an overarching system that includes everything except their own desires. My father experienced this very acutely through being promoted to a position in which he was deathly unhappy. He later returned, very happily, to his original job, where his true skills lay.

Coleridge's attempt at a unity of vision was the natural human reaction to seemingly unrecognizable patterns. His wish was to fit its mesmerizing and wild implacability into a single system that could contain and neutralize its effects.

The wish for unity, for a system, becomes a burden in itself. Before we have looked up from our elaborate Daytimer, the elements with which we grapple have divided around us and joined up to form a world from which the Daytimer itself excludes us. If the organization in effect organizes the complexity and chaos *out* of the system through endless protocol, it is in effect dooming its workers to inevitable decline. An organization that once replicated a living system becomes, without the constant and chaotic reordering necessary for adaptability, a house of the living dead.

STAYING ALIVE AT WORK

"Living systems," according to John Holland, a maverick and inspired student of complexity, "never really settle down." Holland and his colleagues are finding that the plants and animals that do settle down do not survive for very long. It is as if life is forever trying to keep itself exquisitely balanced on the edge between chaos and order, always about to fall into the imprisoning forces of an overly ordered world on one side and the seductive calls of complete chaos on the other. Living systems that survive in the wild, from a flying starling to a rain forest orchid, must learn to adapt with the shifting ecosystems around them, retaining their precarious ecological balance at the vital edge of survival between two competing but necessary worlds. Order and chaos.

A cynic might say that surviving in the wild is easy compared with living in the captivity of an organization. But in the wilderness we have to truly shift for ourselves, whereas in captivity our "meals" are brought to us every day. We do not realize the sophisticated and highly developed skills it takes for any creature to truly live in a wild system. Besides, most of the actual prisons we inhabit we have chosen and furnished ourselves. It is almost impossible for us to admit the extent to which we are held captive by the organization for which we have chosen to work, our self-esteem might not survive that fearless self-appraisal. The study of complexity asks us in effect to open a window and let in fresh air to the organization, to bring a little of the wilderness into the domesticity of the workplace and free us for greater things. When our perceptions have been dulled by the constant wish for order, it may be difficult to imagine a world where we can live at an edge that also includes the patterned chaos of a wild system.

It is astonishing to witness the human ability to shrink from this edge and take on every possible kind of experience in an ordered, burdensome way, as if we could not countenance the possibility of standing upright for a single moment freed from the extra weight of the structures we love to carry with us. A simple love for the purity of the piano becomes a schedule of lessons we can no longer fit into our calendar. A step toward a subject for which we have a passion becomes a costly exercise in college fees and course requirements, only a hundredth part of which contains the simple core that drew us into that sticky, educational spider's lair in the first place. A longed-for increase in salary brings no financial breathing space, but a larger house with the extra burden of its mortgage.

About to begin a new poem, a poet faces the same world. Lifting the pen, the poet carries the whole weight of the world's great literature on his shoulders, including Yeats, Wordsworth, Dickinson, Shakespeare—all the way back through the astonishing angelic calls of Dante to the gritty, disturbing language of *Beowulf*. A poet sits down before the page and wonders how his own imagination, hovering on the unfathomable edge between originality and tradition, can ever be enough in itself.

On my desk, gazing sardonically over my blank page, or at the back of my opened laptop, is a bronze bust of the Irish poet William Butler Yeats. A lyric benchmark of dedication and poetic destiny, he looks over my endeavors through a justifiably arrogant monocle. But the one image of poetic shipwreck, his assured hauteur communicates, is a clear image of the rough shoals of misfortune that await me if I attempt to write like him. Auden said of Yeats, *Proud Ireland hurt you into poetry*. Yeats in turn asks me, with a fierce look from that bronze-monocled eye, "And what, my friend, hurts *you* into poetry?"

When we read Dante or Yeats, we hear and feel textures that are uniquely their own, themselves. Out of a common tradition they shaped a world we would gladly want to join. Yeats had *his* own way, Dante had *his* own way. The tradition tells us again and again that amid the complexities of the world, exactly what we have, exactly our experience, is the only place we can start. Of course, this is just the beginning. Everything must be tested against that same world in which we live; there is a long, hard road to mastery. Whether sitting before the unwritten poem or the yet-to-be-outlined proposal, the sorrow seems to lie in the way we refuse to begin that road. Facing the complexity of everything that has gone before and all that lies ahead, we will not say "enough" to exactly what lies at hand.

The following poem, titled appropriately "Enough," I wrote out of a rare centered spaciousness during a week-long Zen meditation retreat I attended some years ago. Under a strict request not to write or read during the retreat, the swift composition of the poem made it all the more wickedly satisfying and true to its title.

ENOUGH

Enough. These few words are enough.
If not these words, this breath.
If not this breath, this sitting here.
This opening to the life
we have refused
again and again
until now.
Until now.

In this moment of epiphany:

This opening to the life
we have refused

again and again
until now.

It was as if I had caught a delicious scent of something I had long forgotten. A bedrock faith in my own perceptions. How would that dangerous path on the ridge between chaos and order look if I were to say that everything in my life is *enough*, at least to take the next step, to begin? Even, perhaps, the thought that *I could not go on* might be enough. Dante, with his image of waking in a dark wood, reminds us there is a step *even* in that, perhaps especially in that. No one else can experience the feeling that *I cannot take another step* in exactly the same way. That is what must *hurt me* into poetry. This inability to take a step is my own sacred image. My possibility for simplicity in all the complexity. Somehow we are asked to reclaim it as a gift. It opens up, blossoms into something else. We find the door to old and deeper necessities beginning to creak slowly but surely open. We have to crack that door only slightly for the swift breezes alive in the imagination to swing it completely open. Amid the stress and complexity of work, what is it, in Auden's phrase, that *hurts* us into our work?

At the center of a complex and unfathomable world, then, lies our own experience, our own personal history, and our own peculiar way of approach, ready to be tested again and again against unfolding events.

LOST IN THE FOREST

If there is one common experience of complexity in the workplace, it would be the experience of feeling lost. Suddenly coming to our senses amid the blur of events, we realize we are utterly lost in the difficulty of a situation or in our very arrogance or nervousness over a problem. Saying *even this is enough* is the first acceptance of being *lost*, the first simplicity at the center of our work life. But, we ask, wagging our fingers, how does this get the job done? How do we admit to being lost ourselves and yet refuse to be caught in paralysis, self-indulgence, and self-preoccupation?

Poets encounter the same problem. For instance, how to work with the difficult cussed aspects of life without being dragged into a whirlpool of self-pity. Looking over a long line of poets through the ages, it seems to have everything to do with the ability to keep sight of the outer world as we drop down into interior subjective experience. Holding on to the gritty particularities of life even as we delve into deeper levels of self-revelation, we reel out the same golden thread Ariadne passed to Theseus to guide him through the Cretan labyrinth. Attempt to go down without this slight but glowing line back into the world, and we perish, as the self-entangled poets Sylvia Plath and Anne Sexton did, devoured by the minotaur of the self-referential ego. Their poetry had a riveting intensity, but it did not include a greater soul world that could save them from their individual personalities. As Sexton herself wrote of Plath:

> But suicides have a special language
> Like carpenters they want to know which tools.
> They never ask why build.

Knowing *why* we build and *when* to build and *if* to build, then, has a bedrock importance for us. Our lives depend upon it. Especially in a corporate world where few of the underlying assumptions of endless growth and endless endeavor are ever questioned. It can be much more comforting to stay asleep at the wheel and not spoil our momentum or trajectory with disturbing questions.

The marvelous peculiarity about *admitting* to being lost is that we come to our senses. We wake up. We look around with a keenness we did not have before. International Business Machines refused for years to admit to being lost. It could look at the surrounding forest and see only IBM trees, a universe and a market it was sure it had created in its own image. In the sight of the world it served, it was asleep, though the people who managed it were sure they were awake. As I write, IBM is announcing one of the largest quarterly losses in American corporate history—eight billion dollars. The first steps out of this mess must have everything to do with saying "Where, in God's name, are we?"

Here is a poem on the matter of waking up and saving our lives, given by an old Native American elder. The poem is in the form of a story handed down from generation to generation, the kind of story an elder would tell to a young girl or boy whose own life depended on the question, What do I do when I'm lost in the forest? It has been rendered beautifully into modern English by David Wagoner, chair of poetry at the University of Washington. The poem is called "Lost."

It begins in a remarkable and disarming way with the words

> *Stand still. The trees ahead and bushes beside you*
> *Are not lost.*

Here is the full answer David Wagoner hears from the elder's mouth:

> *LOST*
>
> *Stand still. The trees ahead and bushes beside you*
> *Are not lost. Wherever you are is called Here,*
> *And you must treat it as a powerful stranger,*
> *Must ask permission to know it and be known.*
> *The forest breathes. Listen. It answers,*
> *I have made this place around you,*
> *If you leave it you may come back again, saying Here.*

No two trees are the same to Raven.
No two branches are the same to Wren.
If what a tree or a bush does is lost on you,
You are surely lost. Stand still. The forest knows
Where you are. You must let it find you.

The elder reminds us of a consciousness out there in the world, independent of human thought, which can acknowledge us perfectly, just in the place it finds us.

> *. . . Stand still. The forest knows*
> *Where you are. You must let it find you.*

The elder says *we* are not the one to know where our place lies or what action we should take. Put down that burden. We experience those certainties only when we meet the world on its own terms and allow it to find us. IBM had a dire need to put down its own sacrosanct and burdensome image and let the new computer markets speak back and find IBM. But the "expert" mind can never rest enough to allow itself to be found. The elder says that the "I" who places itself at the center of the world will not be the "I" who survives the immensity of the answer. In true creativity, the *expert* hopefully intuits his death.

> *. . . Wherever you are is called Here,*
> *And you must treat it as a powerful stranger,*

Living with complexity, then, has everything to do with paying attention, with looking the world right in the eye even as we are creating our offering, our product, our gift. We not only remain true to our own interior images of desire, but we have enough confidence in them now to test them against the world. To preserve the soulfulness of experience, we pay attention to the world we serve as much as to our own interior life or the interior life of our company. What use our product if there is no place for it to fit? This applies not just to our competitive advantage, but to everything we produce on a planet already choking on an excess of things we might better do without.

> *No two trees are the same to Raven.*
> *No two branches are the same to Wren.*
> *If what a tree or a bush does is lost on you,*
> *You are surely lost.*

A great deal of the exhaustion that comes from work can be attributed to losing sight of the very world we are serving. The excitement that brought us into the endeavor at the beginning may ebb away the more we are enmeshed in the detail. We become enmeshed in the detail because we lose the simplicity that informs the overall pattern of complexity. We lose sight of the wood, in effect, because of the trees; we lose sight of the trees because of our endless self-preoccupation. We not only lose sight of the world that will define our product, we lose a vision of life that helps us to remember we are human souls, living at the center of a troubled and ultimately unfathomable world.

This simple ability to pay attention to the world as we find it may be at the heart of a soulful life worth living, inside or outside the office. Lose your primary entanglement with agonizing beauties of the natural world and you need tremendous lashings of power and money to make up for it. The soul, hungry for belonging, will eat up the whole world if it is bereft of its primary marriage with the trees, sky, and ocean with which it has co-evolved and over millions of years come to love. Yet most people working in the modern corporation are many steps removed from the beauty of the natural world. We might ask, what substitutes can we find? The straight answer is that there are no substitutes. But we also do not need to confine our appreciation of natural processes only to the visual cues we normally associate with "nature," though these may be essential. There is, for instance, tremendous natural "beauty" in an organization that allows people to bloom and grow, to be excited, to be proud of their work, and to understand the connection of the work to a greater ecology than the organization alone.

REMEMBERING THE ESSENTIALS

Sometimes I go about pitying myself,
and all along
my soul is being blown by great winds across the sky.

Ojibway saying

Even as we assure ourselves that money or security is our reason for working, life is continually breaking through our ordered identity to the very edge of chaos, where our hopes for security meet the entangled adventure implicit in living. But much of that entangled adventure does not involve an air ticket or a faraway destination, it has to do with having time for exactly what lies around us. One of the disciplines of building a rich soul life seems to be the simple act, on a daily basis, of remembering what is most important to us. Poets write poetry as much to remember these primary relationships as they do to tell them to others.

This act of remembering can be an uphill struggle. We each have been born and subtly bred into a craze for power and things to an extent that we are constitutionally unable to notice what percentage of our efforts are expended over a lifetime in buying and selling. The corporate world in which we struggle daily for our souls survives on selling endlessly; its culture of adaption is built upon this. We work for, and buy from, enormous engines of production and consumption. Nor are they abstract powers working their evil ways on us. They are an integral part of the world we have created for ourselves. We want them. We cannot even *imagine* a world where people needed less, did with less, and were not under a constant compunction to buy. How would we survive, we ask ourselves? A momentary fall in consumer confidence, a faltering in the very willingness to buy, causes shivers of apprehension in newsrooms around the country. The very act, then, of making a primary soulful entanglement with the world, by really giving it our attention, is a radical and revolutionary step. Having an elemental and intimate relationship with the things of the world instead of wishing to possess them gives us a home at the center of life that is already furnished and paid for.

THE BRIGHT-EYED AND THE LEADEN-EYED

To open up to the world is simply to pay attention to it. Paying attention, we must live up to and into the terrible beauty of what we see. This attention is sustained not only through the classic images and textures of nature around us such as the sun, flocking birds, or spreading trees, but through the newer images of nature constantly being unfolded to us through modern science. It is continually amazing to me, how in the focus on economic realities we are asked to hold at bay any romantic view of our lives, while scientific literature every day uncovers a universe far more astonishing than we could ever draw from myth, fairy story, or our own fancy.

For anyone now reading the poetry of modern science, the universals of life are becoming more and more impossible to ignore. Opening the pages of *Scientific American* and learning about the pulse of a living, breathing, tactile human skin cell or the slow but immense movement of a continental plate around the broad earth's surface, we can almost *feel* the elemental spring, released at the birth of the universe fifteen billion years ago, uncoiling through our everyday existence. Lifting our fingers over the computer keyboard to write a memo, we unconsciously play out the continuing drama of universal existence. A small eddy in the vast river of events, our quickly written memo is a small perturbation on the edge of a vast system, about to change everything or nothing.

Every action taken, from the moment we switch off the alarm clock in the morning to the way we write a line of poetry or design a product, has the potential to change the world, leave it cold with indifference, or, perhaps more commonly, nudge it *infinitesimally* in the direction of good and evil. But we as individual toilers in the companies for which we work tend to see our life in less dramatic terms. Checking through security, we leave the universal laws of pattern, form, and complexity at the door with a numbered ticket. Any company wishing to survive and prosper should be worried about this empty-handed appearance at work. Any individual entering without them should ask themselves why they think the situation demands such a sacrifice.

Leaving the magnificence of the world outside the door, we also leave any desire to really live *in* the world. Our work life, reduced to ashes without the fuel of our deeper personal desires, becomes an unconscious way to commit suicide. The soul bereft of meaningful experience begins to engineer its escape from the structures holding it in check, by dying to itself. The person bereft of imagination interprets the soul's wish literally and begins to look for a full bottle of sleeping tablets. Besides, choosing a gray, loveless life, bereft of the soul's desires, might be the unconscious punishment we seek, having shamefully given up on desire itself. We achieve what seems to be the best and deserved revenge of both worlds, a *living* death played out behind a desk or a sales sheet.

Without a soulful entanglement with the world we experience a poverty that no amount of material reward or recognition will ameliorate. Vachel Lindsay, a now almost forgotten poet who in the early years of this century went from the open road, swapping poems for bread, to the equivalent of a poetic superstar, drawing huge crowds across the cities of America, emphasized the integrity of work combined with the intuition of the universal story of which work is a part. "The Leaden Eyed" takes a hard look at the inner poverty resulting from the refusal to develop that intuition.

THE LEADEN EYED

Let not young souls be smothered out before
They do quaint deeds and fully flaunt their pride.
It is the world's sore crime its babes grow dull,
Its poor are ox-like, limp and leaden eyed.

Not that they starve, but starve so dreamlessly,
Not that they sow, but they seldom reap.
Not that they serve, but have no gods to serve
Not that they die, but that they die like sheep.

THE SECRET OF THE STARLINGS

The interesting thing about the flowing geometries of flocking starlings or the way that organisms evolve and adapt to changing environments is that they do not behave and therefore die like domesticated sheep. Wild sheep perhaps, but not ones held under the watchful crook of a common shepherd. For the starlings, for instance, there is no overarching order which a *flock* follows, only simple elements of behavior that each bird embodies in its own way.

A startlingly clear simulation of this phenomenon was put together by a computer scientist, Craig Reynolds, in 1987. Humorously termed "boids," Reynolds's program attempted to understand, like Coleridge, the flocking abilities of wild birds. The fascinating thing about Reynolds's program is that not once did he include the overarching command "Stay together at all costs."

Reynolds's program depicted a large collection of individual birds, or boids, attempting to fly around a screen full of walls and obstacles. Each boid followed three simple rules of behavior; M. Mitchell Waldrop, in his book *Complexity,* summarizes the three simple behaviors that each boid was programmed to follow:

1. It tried to maintain a minimum distance from other objects in the environment, including other boids.
2. It tried to match velocities with boids in its neighborhood.
3. It tried to move toward the perceived center of mass of boids in its neighborhood.

Waldrop goes on to say:

What was striking about these rules was that none of them said form a flock. Quite the opposite: the rules were entirely local, referring only to what an individual boid could see and do in its own vicinity. If a flock was going to form at all, it was going to have to do so from the bottom up, as an emergent phenomenon. And yet flocks *did* form, every time. Reynolds could start his simulation with boids scattered around his computer screen completely at random, and they would spontaneously collect themselves into a flock that could fly around obstacles in a very fluid and natural manner. Sometimes the flock would even break into subflocks that flowed around both sides of an obstacle, rejoining on the other sides as if the boids had planned it all along. In one of the runs, in fact, a boid accidentally hit a pole, fluttered around for a moment as though stunned and lost, then darted forward to rejoin the flock as it moved on.

Trying to run complex companies, big or small, by imperial command, from the top down, may be *the* single most unnecessary burden carried by any corporate manager. Attempting something that is doomed to fail, they produce a manual of required responses covering all eventualities. Doing this, the system they are forced to employ becomes Byzantine and cumbersome. It also carries an implicit lack of trust in the essential elements of the system—people. Not only that, but hierarchical systems based on power emanating from the top cannot plan for the wild efflorescence of impossible events we call daily life. They are continually immobilized by the changing nature of reality. They lack robustness, adaptability, and in computer simulations with the command "form a flock," instead of flowing lifelike around obstacles, the mass of individual elements moves in the jerky mannerisms of a B-movie dinosaur.

Robert Maxwell, the now-infamous British billionaire tycoon, was an autocrat who played the part of imperial commander as if to the manner born. He astonished even fellow corporate power grabbers by his need to concentrate command solely in his own person or his sons. As his empire grew larger and more Byzantine, it came to the point where no one, perhaps Robert Maxwell least of all, knew what was going on. To fill in the huge fault lines continually appearing across his domains, he threw in everything he could, including the hard-earned pension funds of those who had worked loyally for the very companies that served him.

It might be that anyone refusing to work with the natural constituent elements of a system over time will always be forced to steal from elsewhere to sustain the illusion of omnipotence. My colleague Joel Henning, hero of the *Beowulf* chapter earlier in this book, has a sobering story of an equivalent top-down manipulation that caused devastation to the company which devised it.

The idea, issuing from the boardroom, was to offer tempting prizes and outlandish financial rewards to the one department in the company that could achieve the highest level of growth over the following financial year. Before long it became evident that one particular department had it completely sewn up, and Jim Harrison, the vice president in charge of that area, was the hero of the occasion. By the end of the following financial year his department had doubled its income; no one else came even close to the seductive figures appearing on his reports to the president. Harrison was sent back and forth across the country to give speeches and talks at all the company plants. The toast of the company, by the middle of the following year he had been disgraced and fired.

The success of Jim Harrison was based on the neglect of every constituent part of the system except the one order programmed from above to improve profitability. Rather than being educated into the broad needs of the business, he was manipulated to produce one result at all costs. In his turn he reflected back to upper management an almost Biblical parable of their own narrow vision. To achieve this, his department had dropped all its education and training programs, stopped all new hiring, cut its research and development to the bone, and instilled the chill atmosphere of a police state onto the office floor. In the second year Harrison's department *lost* money at a greater rate than any other department. His people were leaving in droves despite the glittering prizes of the previous year, he had trained no one to replace them, and there were no new products appearing on the horizon for them to sell.

This is a true but almost cartoonlike representation of small-mindedness. The dynamics we face are almost always more subtle and more finely balanced, yet the elements with which we engage at work are invariably the same. Our hope is to stop the world for one half-second so that we can get on, and perhaps, for that one precious moment, get a glimpse of a place to which we can truly belong. We want to isolate one part of the onward flow and clasp it to our breasts. The hope, like an arrow through the heart, is achingly human, but the grab for power to stop the broad, flowing onrush of events honors anything *but* our humanity.

The new science of complexity echoes the wisdom long passed down in the poetic tradition. The way to build a poem or a lifelike and useful system is to fold meaning into the simplest elements and allow complexity to emerge from their natural self-generation. Deal with many simple elements instead of one complex system. Think locally, *act* locally, *intuit* globally. Once in a *very* blue moon the world allows us the God-given right to actually *act* globally, but the opportunity occurs more rarely than we would wish. We simply have less wisdom than the emergent intelligence of many individuals, given enough information and the ability to act. For instance, if there are funds for wages, tell the work team how much there is available for that cost and let them pay themselves. Always let them keep some of what they make above and beyond their costs. Let them have a say in the hiring of team members. In an organization, let the behavior emerge from the bottom up instead of the top down. "And while you are at it," Waldrop quotes Chris Langton, a longtime student of artificial life, "focus on emergent behavior instead of the final result."

Breathless and arrogant with the universal elements I have uncovered in this chapter, I might add some other free advice to Langton's while the heat of enthusiasm is upon me. *Ergo*, for those attempting to travel with others across our now-troubled corporate landscape: Stop treating people as if they are dangerous vehicles about to spin out of control unless you are constantly applying the brakes. Educate them into everything you know, ask them to learn more than you know. Show them not only how to find the brake but the accelerator as well. If their driving style is different, make sure they stop for red lights and know the rules of the road. If they don't like the justice of the road or the rules, let them attempt their own roads and their own rules. Be surprised. Let them experience failure if there is the least room for maneuver. Let them experience *you* experiencing failure with or without the least room for maneuver. Act as if your own internal soul images matter, and out of that surety stand in awe of what arises from the imaginations of others. Above all, have faith in those elements of the universe, nourishing or poisonous, that have *honored* you with their proximity. Do *not* form a flock!

The Soul of the World

Toward an Ecological Imagination

Perhaps the truth depends upon a walk

around the lake. —WALLACE STEVENS

Though our self-preoccupation is endless, and corporation or career the central fixation of our lives, if we do not take into account the greater soul of the world which sustains our endeavors, and from which we take our resources, nothing I have said about our personal struggles in the workplace can apply.

There is a core delusion at the center of our struggles in all organizations. A core delusion that narrows our sense of self and ignores the greater world beyond the organization. It is a world that can inform us of our personal destiny, but also a world that we have lost the time and inclination to investigate thoroughly. Trying to ignore this greater world, we forge a small identity held within the narrow corridors of the building in which we work. Rather than breathing life and vitality into work from the greater perspective which is our birthright, we allow our dreams and desires to be constricted and replaced by those of the organization and then wonder why it has such a stranglehold on our lives.

The first step to preserving the soul in our individual lives is to admit that the world has a soul also, and is somehow participating with us in our work and destiny. That there is a sacred otherness to the world which is breathtakingly helpful simply because it is not us; it is not defined by our human worries and preoccupations, and it never will be. Its refusal to concern itself solely with our personal ambitions is its greatest mercy; it reserves itself for another kind of nourishment, one we come to when we are ready to drop our reflexive self-concern and look beyond our exhausting self-importance. As the poet David Ignatow reminds himself:

> *I should be content*
> *to look at a mountain*
> *for what it is*
> *and not as a comment on my life.*

Looking at the mountain for it own sake opens up a life that can be described only in the numinous effulgence of poetry or the self-forgetfulness of vital prose. This self-forgetfulness is the essence of firsthand experience. We no longer see our experience as useful for getting something out of *someone* else, or getting us quickly *somewhere* else, but as the primary touchstone of both our individuality and the strange way our individuality depends upon everything else. In such experience there is nowhere to go because the experience of interdependence is complete in itself. This experience of belonging satisfies a primary hunger that lies at the center of our soul life; it holds both restful and fiery qualities simultaneously, it is not an easy out. Taking the first vulnerable steps into our own experience, no matter how small or hidden at the beginning, opens us to a more generous life, where what we have to give figures as largely as what we receive. We stop trying to draw infinitely from a finite world and begin to learn how little is necessary to live a life that honors the soul of the world. We learn that in many respects our world works as a partner, sometimes friendly, sometimes terrifying, but always true to its own necessities and by its example drawing us toward our own.

In *A Far-off Place*, Laurens Van Der Post speaks movingly of these necessities and forces that shape our lives, and the sacramental nature of our involvement through the still-participative eyes of the Kalahari Bushmen.

Remember . . . that no matter how awful and insignificant, how ugly or beautiful it might look to you, everything in the bush has its own right to be there. No one can challenge this right unless compelled by some necessity of life itself. Everything has its own dignity, however absurd it might seem to you, and we are all bound to recognize and respect it as we wish our own life to be recognized and accepted. Life in the bush is necessity, and it understands all forms of necessity. It will always forgive what is imposed upon it out of necessity, but it will never understand and accept any less than necessity . . . remember that every-

*where it has its own watchers to see whether the law of neces-
sity is being observed. . . .*

But this life of necessity must now be achieved outside the Kalahari, in the landscape of the postmodern
corporation. No matter how narrow our perceptions
become in the daily obsessions of the organization,
there is no such thing as a life lived only within a
corporation. There are other necessities calling us to
a much greater participation than any corporation
can offer. The most efficiently run, streamlined organization, the best-groomed, most-organized executive, is interwoven with the ragged vagaries of
creation, and despite our best attempts to anchor ourselves in the concrete foundations of profitability and
permanence, we remain forever at the whim, mercy,
and pleasure of the windblown world.

Ironically, we bring more vitality into our organizations when we refuse to make their goals the measure of our success and start to ask about the greater
goals they might serve, and when we stop looking to
them as parents who will supply necessities we can
only obtain when we wrestle directly with our own
destiny.

In a sense, we place the same burdens on our organizational life as we place on the rest of our existence.
We feel there is something wrong at the center of it
all, and we have to put it right. We are forever looking
for a cure for our ills. We do this by placing ourselves
in the position of *manager*, of thus *managing* change.

Unless it is managed, something is wrong. But our real unconscious and underlying wish is to find a cure for the impermanence of life, and for that there is no remedy. Most of the difficulties we confront at work are no different from those human beings have been dealing with for millennia. Life is full of loneliness, failure, grief and loss to an extent that terrifies us, and we will do anything to will ourselves another existence.

THE INNER VOICE AND THE OUTER WORLD

The impulse is to force perfection upon ourselves and climb straight up the mountain toward our vision of heaven. Helen Luke, author of *Dark Wood to White Rose*, a marvelous companion book to Dante's *Commedia*, looks at Dante's early wish in the poem to circumvent the necessary visit to hell and ascend to heaven directly. As if attempting to leave the body through the head by *thinking* his way into his happiness. Ignoring the need to go beneath the surface of existence, he started to climb straight up the side of the nearest mountain. Very soon he found three fearsome beasts blocking his path: the lion, the leopard, and the wolf. To the medieval mind unaccustomed to Sierra Club calendars and the Discovery Channel, these were very clear signs. Dante saw the lion as his own disowned courage projected out as aggression and inner pride, the wolf as his greed, always on the move, and the leopard as the fast-moving part of the mind that stalks life as prey, called in medieval times, with great relish, *lust*. Dante turns back, unable to pass the very parts of himself that he had hoped to leave behind. "We may thank God," says Luke. "It is when we admit our powerlessness that the guide appears."

The man who does appear to guide Dante through the gates of hell is the poet Virgil. Virgil is a voice we come to recognize in the end as our very own, and which keeps us company through the shadows of existence as we enter deeper and deeper into the life we desire for ourselves. It becomes Dante's task to follow this voice, first learning its demands and advice, then becoming its companion, and finally melding with it until it becomes his own. All this in preparation to meet the divine representation of feminine love in the form of Beatrice.

As Virgil stands before Dante, he does not raise his finger and lecture Dante in any way. He shows him the gate to hell and the words written above: "Lay down all hope, you that go in by me."

The hope that Dante is asked to lay down is the hope for immunity. Immunity from his own shadows and from the greater life glinting and winking at him from every direction. Through this gate he will experience all the parts of himself he feels are inferior to his needs, and all the newborn lives he had smothered before they could disturb his stable delusions. In short, the most fearful parts of ourselves that we as human beings hide but must eventually confront.

In the outer institutional world (another, more concrete form of hell) we can feel the weblike imprisonment of the organization's shadow as the very place where our own disowned and rejected sides entangle and enmesh themselves, and the very place where it is the most difficult to admit them. Stuck to the corporate tar baby and too busy to find time for a greater perspective, we substitute the organization for a much more embracing and universal experience of life and exhaust ourselves on its narrow aims. Each one of us at one time or another has seen those letters of fire written invisibly above our office door: "Lay down all hope, you that go in by me." Of course, by the time we have earned our own office, hell has become a very familiar place. Matt Groening's "Life in Hell" cartoon astutely depicts the family as the place where "hell" is first experienced. As adults, the institution or the corporation becomes the family once again, and we gladly assume our roles in its system, forgetting that as children we learned to play our inherited family role to the death. Recognizing we have returned to our family hell again, we try to exempt ourselves from it by assuming a professional demeanor and hide our immature parts by presenting the smooth face and the smooth life. Like our early trauma in our own family, we feel that failure and vulnerability may mean being cast out of the circle— the only one we know—into the outer darkness. For many of us, then, it can be an immense step simply to admit to the presence of this darker cycle within us. To admit our own dark side is to admit that there is a possibility of not belonging.

THE CYCLES. ALL THE OTHER CYCLES.

Until we take this step into the lower half of the cycle of experience, half our power and potential remains behind. The extent to which we exclude the shadowy, failing sides of ourselves from the workplace is the extent to which one half of us is hidden. At bottom, we distrust the cyclical nature of living and dying. In the poem "For/From Lew," Gary Snyder imagines what his old close friend, Lew Welch, would say if he could bring himself back to life and tell those whom he had left behind why he had taken his own life.

> *"There's a basic fear between your world and*
> *mine. I don't know why.*
> *What I came to say was,*
> *teach the children about the cycles.*
> *The life cycles. All the other cycles.*
> *That's what it's all about, and it's all forgot."*

This forgetting is an almost unconscious gap in our "knowledge." If the phone rings and a friend asks us to jump in the car and spend some time in the city tonight, we do not look out the window at the night sky and say, "I'm sorry, but I just don't leave the house in the last half of the month, when the moon is growing smaller, I go out only in the first part of the month, when the moon is growing larger, and oh, yes, I certainly do not go out of the house for those three nights when there is no moon at all, it's all too scary."

If we did say this in reply to an evening's invitation, our friend might think we were going insane, yet it is exactly this insanity that prevents us from bringing a fuller measure of ourselves into the workplace. We think we exist only when our life looks like the first half of the cycle, when our "moon" is waxing, when our sense of ourselves is growing and getting larger, when we are succeeding or stepping up to the line for promotion. If things are dying or falling away, we dismiss it, we refuse to see it as the second half of the very same cycle and think there is something "wrong" with us. We think something terrible has happened and we need to do a whole list of things to put it right. Much of our stress and subsequent exhaustion at work comes from our wish to keep ourselves at full luminescence all month, even when our interior "moon" may be just a sliver in the sky, or about to fade from sight altogether. It takes tremendous energy to keep up a luminescent front when the interior surface is fading into darkness. In some ways we are constantly preventing our own rebirth into new cycles and greater lives, and instead work twenty-four hours a day keeping a wraithlike image of our former selves alive long after its time has past. This "night of the living dead" syndrome is just as true of an organization as it is of a person. We spend enormous amounts of energy investing in structures that would gladly leave us if we could only let them go.

It is as if Dante were to say to Virgil, "This is an important path for me to tread, but these are my terms, I want a signed agreement that you won't take me anywhere where I can stumble and fall, or anywhere where it is really dark. No moonless nights, thank you." Yes, we say, I want the destiny that awaits me, but I want complete safety while I explore it.

We might think of the moon as being the natural cyclical reminder of our own internal ebb and flow. The wish to keep the moon full all month, imposing our will on the body of the heavens, is the wish to stay in the addicting and forever-youthful light of masculine "peak performance." This phenomenon was played out forcefully in the early nineteen-seventies. Women moving into positions of greater power and responsibility in the workplace found enormous suspicion of the female menstrual cycle and its effect on others. Managers were repeatedly quoted saying they did not wish their offices in chaos at certain times of the month. Whatever the focus of our suspicions, there is tremendous pressure in the modern business world to ignore the changing cycles of our native energies. As I mention earlier, the greatest proportion of heart attacks in North America occur between eight A.M. and nine A.M. on Monday mornings. Most of these victims are men, at the low point of a weekly cycle. It is as if the human frame is at its most vulnerable facing the prospect of another week keeping the inner celestial reflector at full luminescence.

I found myself confronting the image of the moon in a short poem called "Faith," written when I had very little reflected light, just a sliver of a moon to see by.

> *I want to write about faith*
> *about the way the moon rises*
> *over cold snow, night after night,*
>
> *faithful even as it fades from fullness,*
> *slowly becoming that last curving and impossible*
> *sliver of light before the final darkness.*
>
> *But I have no faith myself*
> *I refuse it the smallest entry.*
>
> *Let this then, my small poem,*
> *like a new moon, slender and barely open,*
> *be the first prayer that opens me to faith.*

Poetry is the art of overhearing ourselves say things from which it is impossible to retreat. A true line acts like a lightning rod in a storm. All our doubts about the reality of the experience disappear in a flash as the accumulated charge contained in the electric ripeness of the moment runs to earth. Just before we are struck, we may even feel, as in a true lightning storm, the hair rising on the back of the neck, as we realize "it" is being said . . .

> *. . . the way the moon rises*
> > *over cold snow, night after night,*
>
> *faithful even as it fades from fullness,*

What I overheard in "Faith" was a question I wasn't sure I wanted to hear, in a voice that demanded an answer. "What would my life be like if I had as much faith in the parts of me that were fading away as I had in the parts of me that were growing?"

The soulful approach to work admits and allows the yeast of loss into our work lives. Embracing loss, we begin to understand the necessity of failure, and in the possibility of failure begin to understand the magnificence of even the humblest human path. We accept that the stakes are high for everyone living in "the organization," and that we live in a greater universal "organization" that stretches beyond the office door to the limits of human experience. We come to accept that every one of us can fail, fail to live the life we desire for ourselves, or even fail to uncover the desire itself. Without failure we have no possibility of appreciating or praising the life well lived, the work well done, a place well taken care of, or the greater ecology that makes up our home.

THE ECOLOGICAL IMAGINATION

Releasing ourselves from the need to keep half of ourselves hidden, we can begin to bring these other neglected sides into the workplace, to entertain the possibility that there is an integral wholeness to all the seemingly antagonistic and opposing sides of ourselves, a possibility that we may not have to be "fixed" or amended before we can serve ourselves or the company. "A first step," as the philosopher Gregory Bateson put it, "towards an Ecology of Mind."

The abiding image of a diverse and rich ecology is the Amazon rain forest. As human beings, we look at the rain forest and see an ecology made up of thousands of species that fit together exquisitely. The image is so satisfying to us, because when we see the forest and all the disparate forms, odors, and cries that make it up, we intuit a life where all our own strange and eccentrically exotic parts can fit too. A place where the cross-grain of experience makes not a disconnect, but a mysterious embracing pattern. A balanced, intricate ecology, in effect, asks us to stop choosing between parts of ourselves according to what we think belongs and what does not. A mature ecology needs its microscopic leaf molds as much as its panthers. It does not make a choice between them, saying, "I'll take three dozen of those gorgeous panthers and cancel the tacky leaf molds." If it did, the rain forest would soon, as the metaphor goes, be out of business. No leaf molds, no compost, no compost, no life.

In a way, we put our sense of self out of business because much of our education has been bent toward raising us not as an intricate ecology of qualities but as a monoculture where our own internal leaf molds are eradicated from our self-identity in the name of drying us out, tidying us up, and making us presentable for the great economic system that awaits us. A great deal of our education is based on removing our faith in the fading half of the cycle of existence, and the chief tool for removing our faith is shame. We are slowly but surely told that great parts of us do not belong in the classroom. Only certain parts of us are required to attend, almost always the parts that learn how the status quo works. The parts that think for themselves, or are allied with the ability to die as well as grow, tend to cause trouble, and with a little effort can eventually be discouraged from showing up. As adults, these same parts of us stay out in the parking lot while we climb out of the car in the morning and head toward the revolving door of the building. The person left out in the car is often a part we once treasured: a person awestruck with wonder, ripe with the dumbest questions, and thirsting to learn. I remember my very first science class at Mirfield Grammar School. To begin my scientific career, my science teacher asked me to name a few elements. I was so excited, I shouted back immediately, "Earth, Air, Fire, and Water." An elemental and enthusiastic offering and a great place to begin a discussion of the classical scientific world view, one would think. But no, apparently an opportunity for ridicule. I soon learned to keep quiet with this man, hiding my enthusiasm, and narrowing my identity in his presence, but luckily found opportunities to blossom with other more curious teachers who inhabited the school. It's not always possible if we are completely surrounded by the living dead.

In effect, instead of building a complex ecology that lives magnificently, generation to generation, in a kind of massive ongoing self-recycling, we plant a single crop, a single set of ambitions inside us, one which is replicated inside everyone else, and one which, like our monocultural agricultural systems, needs massive amounts of outside energy to stay healthy. Instead of a marvelous identity made up of thousands of scents, cries, ferns, trees, animals, and multicolored birds, we say, "I am wheat and only wheat. My teacher wanted wheat, my boss wants wheat, *wheat* is what you get." But to grow wheat, fencerow to fencerow like this, we have to pour onto the land a continual stream of hydrocarbons and spray down massive amounts of poison to keep the system from blighting itself.

The outside energy that keeps us "alive" can take many forms. Money, promotions, promises, benefits, or the multi-billion-dollar prescription drug industry that helps keep us "going" when our own health fails. More innocently, it can take the form of endless cups of coffee, sleeping pills, sugar, aspirin, or less innocently the deadlier drugs that seeped into American work life in the seventies—the poison unfortunately we administer to ourselves, the constant daily drip of self-criticism that reinvents and justifies all the reasons we are not good enough, and all the ways we do not deserve the life we desire.

We must ask ourselves, if it takes so much energy and so much constant drive, and if it takes tremendous amounts of "poison" to stop parts of me from rising up and taking back my life again, what kind of work am I involved in? Why do I think it necessary to hide from myself for most of the day?

COMING OUT OF HIDING

Preserving the soul means that we come out of hiding at last and bring more of ourselves into the workplace. *Especially* the parts that do not "belong" to the company. In a sense, the very part of us that doesn't have the least interest in the organization is our greatest offering to it. It is the part that opens the window of the imagination and allows fresh air into the meeting room. It is the part that can put its foot on the brake when the organization is running itself off a cliff. It's the part that can identify unethical behavior and remind everyone what the real priorities are. It is the part that refuses to shame itself or others in order to make its way through the organization. In short, its identity is not locked into the very fears that stop an organization from having the perspectives and adaptability to save itself.

If an organization can gain the perspective to save

itself from its own collective death wish, how much more so an individual human being? A single human being has all the benefits and gifts of her own native intelligence, her own imagination, and her own intuition to guide her through the difficulties. Not only this, but men and women have the timeless human capacity for a religious soul experience of life that an organization cannot. Human beings have an intuitive capacity and knowledge (what the romantic poets called *sensibility*) that somewhere at the center of life is something ineffably and unalterably right and good, and that this "rightness" can be discovered through artistic and spiritual explorations that have been honored by all the great perennial religious traditions.

The perennial traditions tell us that despite the impermanent aspect of existence, there is nothing wrong with the world or the things that make it up. They tell us that we are not the center of the universe except in those exquisite moments when the universe in its wisdom chooses to have us be so. Discovering we are not the center of creation becomes a blessed release and a marvelous unburdening. It allows us to meet creation on its own terms, to see it as a continuing form of revelation rather than a source of disappointment when it does not make our career a number-one priority. The burden of creativity is the burden of identity. Meeting creation on its own terms, we are able to stop our interminable self-preoccupied monologue for one precious moment and hear creation speaking to someone greater and larger than the person indicated by our job descriptions. We are not our job descriptions, and the small, confining prisons those descriptions have made for us. We are not our profit and loss statement. Nor are we our ambitions and career prospects. As the Chinese sage Wu Wei Wu admonished:

> *Why are you unhappy?*
> *Because 99.9% of what you think,*
> *And everything you do,*
> *Is for your self,*
> *And there isn't one.*

Why is the present corporation such a desperate well of anxiety and stress? Because all its strivings are to preserve its identity for the future, and for the most part it doesn't have an identity, or at least one the soul might consider worth wanting. Oscar Wilde's ironic summation about someone he knew, "He has no enemies but is intensely disliked by all his friends," could be said about our societal relationship with corporate America. We have been handed an accepted work world in which the things that really matter in human life have been pushed to the margins of our culture. Much of our present struggles with our organizations have to do with remembering what is essential and placing it back in the center of our lives. We stop waiting in quiet desperation for our career rewards to

get to a point where they finally make up to us everything we have lost.

In a very real way, the old corporate world now
passing away had become for us a form of ritual, almost religious life. Like many quasi-religious movements that have ultimately failed to make us a home
in the world, corporate America tried to offer us another form of transcendence from the difficulties of
the body and the complexities of the natural world. It
required many of the sacrifices that religions preoc-
cupied with hierarchy have demanded. It asked us to
give up our own desires, to pay no heed to our bodily
experience, to think abstractly, to put organizational
goals above home and family, and, like many institutional religions, it asked us not to be troubled by any
questionable activity; corporate America, after all,
stood for a greater good.

Preserving the soul in corporate America means
reclaiming all those human soul qualities sacrificed
on the altar of organizational survival. In the very
act of reclaiming them, the personal interior struggle
becomes an outer political action. There is nothing
more transforming to the American workplace than
the thousands of daily decisions now being made that
put soul life above the abstracts of organizational life.
Many people now refuse the wrenching transfers to
faraway cities that were formerly necessary to advancement. Many ignore the constant demands for
more and more of the time that robs their families of
their presence. Even those who continue to sacrifice

in this way are asking questions aloud in the workplace that a short few years ago could be said only in desperation to strangers in a bar. Those corporations riding the wave of this change are the ones that understand this birthright reclamation on the part of their employees as being just as necessary for the corporation as it is for the individuals who make it up.

The new organization that honors the soul and the soul of the world will be what Peter Senge has called the "learning organization," an organization that is as much concerned with what it serves as what it is, as much attentive to the greater world as the small world it has become, as much trying to learn from the exquisite patterns that inform that greater world as trying to impose its own pattern on something already complete. It would be an organization willing to ask deeply radical questions about whether its products are actually *necessary*. A soul-based organization would have Zen Master Suzuki Roshi's quality of *beginner's mind*, the willingness to look at the world as if for the first time and honor and emulate its ability to present astonishing sophistication in the simplest of forms.

The organization that has made room for the soul learns slowly and painfully that clinging to premature and constricted identities restricts the flow of energy from outside the system it has created. Constricted by monochromatic images of how things should be, people, talent, and money all have a hard time leaving and entering. A constricted identity puts too much focus on boundaries that tell us what is familiar and what is not. But a focus on the interior vastness of beingness itself creates a strong sense of self without having to delineate the barriers in advance.

This emphasis on the vastness of human experience, stretching far beyond the walls of the corporation and its helpless preoccupations with power, money, and sales, blunts our acquisitive nature and allows us to join the concerns of our workplace with the concerns of our world. The soul of the world makes its revelations felt not by lecturing us that there is something wrong with our endless wanting, but by giving us glimpses of a numinous experience of life that stops our wanting in its tracks, because in that state we simply do not require anything else to complete ourselves, except, perhaps, the one continuing desire of all desires, to bring that vital celebration of experience into the center of our existence. For many, this is the power of God's presence in their lives. God him- or herself becomes the signifying focus for the sacred otherness of the world. For those who do not see their life experience through a traditional religious framework, it is the language or symbol they use to describe what is most precious to them, and what in the greater scheme of things they have chosen to serve.

I do not believe that there is a possibility of preserving the soul in the workplace without this essential link with what we have chosen to serve. But I also do not believe we can interpret service as the complete surrender of personal desire. It is exactly through desire that we discover what animates and moves us. As I say earlier in the book, if we do surrender our desires too early in the process, we very soon find ourselves controlled by those who have kept their own desires alive. To preserve our deeper desires amid the pressures of the modern corporation is to preserve our souls for the greater life we had in mind when we first took the job.

The rich flow of creativity, innovation, and almost musical complexity we are looking for in a fulfilled work life cannot be reached through trying or working harder. The medium, for the soul, it seems, must be the message. The river down which we raft is made up of the same substance as the great sea of our destination. An ever-moving first-hand creative engagement with life and with others that completes itself simply by *being* itself. This kind of approach must be seen as the "great art" of working *in order* to live, of remembering what is most important in the order of priorities, and what place we occupy in a much greater story than the one our job description defines. Other "great arts," such as poetry, can remind and embolden us to this end. Whatever we choose to do, the stakes are very high. With a little more care, a little more courage, and, above all, a little more soul, our lives can be so easily discovered and celebrated in work, and not, as now, squandered and lost in its shadow.

Bibliography

CHAPTER 1. The Path Begins: Inviting the
Soul to Work

Blake, William. *William Blake* (The Oxford Authors), ed. Michael Mason. Oxford University Press, 1988.

Claremont de Castillejo, Irene. *Knowing Woman, A Feminine Psychology.* Harper Colophon Books, 1974.

Dante Alighieri. *The Comedy of Dante Alighieri, the Florentine,* trans. Dorothy Sayers and Barbara Reynolds. Penguin Books, 1949.

Gioia, Dana. *Can Poetry Matter?* Gray Wolf Press, 1992. First appeared in *Atlantic Monthly* magazine. May, 1991.

Hillman, James. *A Blue Fire.* Harper & Row, 1989.

Luke, Helen. *Dark Wood to White Rose: Journey and Transformation in Dante's Divine Comedy.* Parabola, 1989.

Paglia, Camille. *Sexual Personae.* Vintage Books, 1991.

Stevens, Wallace. *Collected Poems.* Alfred A. Knopf, 1955.

Storr, Anthony. *Solitude: A Return to the Self.* Ballantine, 1988.

Williams, William Carlos. *The Collected Poems of William Carlos Williams, 1939–1962, Vol. II.* New Directions, 1962.

Wordsworth, William. *William Wordsworth* (The Oxford Authors), ed. Stephen Gill. Oxford University Press, 1988.

Yevtushenko, Yevgeny. *Selected Poems*, trans. R. R. Milner-Gulland and Peter Levi. Penguin Books, 1962.

CHAPTER 2. Beowulf: Power and Vulnerability in the Workplace

Blake, William. *William Blake* (The Oxford Authors), ed. Michael Mason. Oxford University Press, 1988.

Bly, Robert, ed. *News of the Universe: Poems of Twofold Consciousness*. Sierra Club Books, 1980.

Boyle, Nicholas. *Goethe: The Poet and the Age, Vol. I: The Poetry of Desire*. Oxford University Press, 1991.

Eliot, T. S. *Collected Poems, 1909–1962*. Harcourt Brace Jovanovich, 1963.

Raffel, Burton, trans. *Beowulf*. New American Library, 1963.

Rilke, Rainer Maria. *Selected Poems*, trans. Robert Bly. Harper & Row, 1981.

Rilke, Rainer Maria. *The Selected Poetry of Rainer Maria Rilke*, trans. Stephen Mitchell. Vintage Books, 1984.

Swearer, Randolph, et al. *Beowulf: A Likeness*. Yale University Press, 1990.

CHAPTER 3. Fire in the Earth: Toward a Grounded Creativity

Block, Peter. *The Empowered Manager*. Jossey–Bass, 1987.

Bolen, Jean Shinola, M.D. *Goddesses in Everywoman: A New Psychology of Women.* Harper Colophon Books, 1985.

Frost, Robert. *The Poetry of Robert Frost.* Holt, Rinehart and Winston, 1969.

Hirshfield, Jane, and Mariko Aratani, trans. *The Ink Dark Moon.* Random House, 1990.

Machado, Antonio. *Times Alone: Selected Poems of Antonio Machado,* trans. Robert Bly. Wesleyan University Press, 1983.

Neruda, Pablo. *Selected Poems,* ed. Nathaniel Tarn. Penguin Books, 1975.

Rinpoche, Sogyal. *The Tibetan Book of Living and Dying.* HarperCollins, 1992.

CHAPTER 4. Fire in the Voice: Speaking Out at Work

Ackerman, Diane. *A Natural History of the Senses.* Vintage Books, 1991.

Blake, William. *William Blake* (The Oxford Authors), ed. Michael Mason. Oxford University Press, 1988.

Burns, Robert. *Poems and Songs.* Gordon Wright Publishing, 1989.

Eliot, T. S. *Collected Poems, 1909–1962.* Harcourt Brace Jovanovich, 1963.

Rilke, Rainer Maria. *Selected Poems,* trans. Robert Bly. Harper & Row, 1981.

CHAPTER 5. Fionn and the Salmon of Knowledge: Innocence and Experience in Corporate America

Blake, William. *William Blake* (The Oxford Authors), ed. Michael Mason. Oxford University Press, 1988.

Dames, Michael. *Mythic Ireland*. Thames and Hudson, 1992.

Ellis, Peter Berresford. *Celtic Inheritance*. Muller, 1985.

MacCana, Proinsias. *Celtic Mythology*. Peter Bedrick Books, 1987.

Oliver, Mary. *New and Selected Poems, 1992*. Atlantic Monthly Press, 1992.

Stephens, James. *The Crock of Gold*. 1912.

Yeats, William Butler. *The Poetry of W. B. Yeats*. Macmillan, 1983.

CHAPTER 6. Taking the Homeward Road: The Soul at Midlife

Chinen, Allan. *Once Upon a Midlife*. Tarcher, 1992.

Eliot, T. S. *Collected Poems, 1909–1962*. Harcourt Brace Jovanovich, 1963.

Estes, Clarissa Pinkola. *Women Who Run with the Wolves*. Ballantine. 1992.

Machado, Antonio. *Times Alone: Selected Poems of Antonio Machado*, trans. Robert Bly. Wesleyan University Press, 1983.

Ritsos, Yannis. *Exile and Return. Selected Poems, 1967–1974*, trans. Edmund Keeley. Ecco Press, 1985.

Schumacher, E. F. *Good Work*. Jonathan Cape, 1979.

Walcott, Derek. *Sea Grapes*. Farrar, Straus & Giroux, 1976.

CHAPTER 7. Coleridge and Complexity: Facing What Is Sweet and What Is Terrible

Auden, W. H. *The English Auden: Poems, Essays and*

Dramatic Writings, ed. Edward Mendelson. Random House, 1977.

Autry, James A. *Love and Profit: The Art of Caring Leadership*. William Morrow and Co., 1991.

Basho. *On Love and Barley: Haiku of Basho*, trans. Lucien Stryk. Penguin Books, 1985.

Bennis, Warren. *Why Leaders Can't Lead*. Jossey-Bass, 1989.

Briggs, John, and David Peat. *Turbulent Mirror: An Illustrated Guide to Chaos Theory and the Science of Wholeness*. Harper & Row, 1989.

Coleridge, S. T. *Samuel Taylor Coleridge* (The Oxford Authors), ed. H. J. Jackson. Oxford University Press, 1985.

Covey, Stephen. *Principle-Centered Leadership*. Summit Books, 1991.

Gill, Stephen. *William Wordsworth: A Life* (Oxford Lives). Oxford University Press, 1989.

Gleick, James. *Chaos: Making a New Science*. Viking Penguin, 1987.

Holmes, Richard. *Coleridge: Early Visions*. Viking Penguin, 1989.

Perkins, David. *A History of Modern Poetry*. Belknap Press, 1987.

Wagoner, David. *Who Shall Be the Sun?* University of Indiana Press, 1978.

Waldrop, M. Mitchell. *Complexity*. Simon & Schuster, 1992.

Wheatley, Margaret J. *Leadership and the New Science*. Berrett-Koehler, 1992.

Yeats, William Butler. *The Poetry of W. B. Yeats*. Macmillan, 1983.

CHAPTER 8. The Soul of the World: Toward an
Ecological Imagination

Bateson, Gregory. *Steps to an Ecology of Mind.* Ballantine, 1972.

Bly, Robert, ed. *News of the Universe.* Sierra Club Books, 1980.

Daly, Herman, and John Cobb. *For the Common Good: Redirecting the Economy Toward Community, the Environment and a Sustainable Future.* Beacon Press, 1989.

Luke, Helen. *Dark Wood to White Rose: Journey and Transformation in Dante's Divine Comedy.* Parabola, 1989.

Shepard, Paul. *Madness and Nature.* Sierra Club Books, 1982.

Senge, Peter. *The Fifth Discipline.* Doubleday/Currency, 1990.

Snyder, Gary. *Ax Handles.* North Point Press, 1963.

Van Der Post, Laurens. *A Far-Off Place.* William Morrow and Company, 1967.

Whyte, David. *Where Many Rivers Meet.* Many Rivers Press, 1989.

Permissions

Index

CURRENCY

DOUBLEDAY